Learning To Liberty

by Stephanie Morgan

Wholesale discounts for book orders are available through Ingram Distributors.

ISBN
978-1-988186-38-2 (softcover)
978-1-988186-39-9 (ebook)

Published in Canada.

First Edition

Table of Contents

Part 1

Part 2

Dedicated to the wonderful horses and people who have helped shape who I am today. Without your love, patience, and the constant new challenges and opportunities you offered me, I would have never gotten this far. For that I am forever grateful. Thank you.

— STEPHANIE MORGAN

Part 1

I DON'T HAVE TOO MANY MEMORIES OF A TIME BEFORE horses. My family lived in a small house with a fair-sized back-yard. My brothers and I lived close enough to walk to school and there were two parks nearby to play at. Cedarvale Crescent was a quiet little street but a lot of the kids who lived there were my age. This gave the neighbourhood a club feeling. In the evenings, only before dark of course, we'd play on the street. Our favourite game was kick-the-can, which is basically like tag with a can as home base. If you got past the person who was "it" and kicked the can over, you would win the game. The person who was "it" would then have to be "it" again. Unfortunately, I was not a very athletic kid, and so I was "it" often. Now I joke about how baseball is the game I hate - I cannot run fast, I cannot throw far, and I most definitely cannot catch something that is coming towards me.

To make matters worse, I was incredibly shy. Being shy and not at all athletic often translated to the other kids as being "dumb". Years later, my self-confidence is still something I need to work on and try to improve on a day-to-day basis. It's gotten better.

Who would have thought that a girl like me would turn into a determined horse trainer and inspiring riding coach? Not me. Not until I turned 12, anyway.

People say that liking horses is almost a disease: you get bit by the bug and all of sudden you can't stop thinking about them. When I was a baby my parents' house had backed onto a race track; perhaps I was bitten quite early. But I didn't get to take lessons until much later.

At the age of eight I had a best friend. In retrospect Olivia was probably just an older girl on the block with a lot of patience who didn't have the heart to say no to me. Olivia took riding lessons. While laying across her bed surrounded by artwork of horses - beautiful, big, majestic horses - she would tell me about how Daisy had taken off with her or had tried to eat the grass while they were trotting on a trail ride. As I listened to her stories, it didn't take long for me to become completely fascinated with horses.

When I was around nine or ten we moved to a larger city. I had been begging my parents like crazy to start riding lessons, or even just to go pet the horses - I would have done anything just to see one in real life. I'd gone on pony rides at the St. Jacobs Farmers' market as many times as they would allow, but after we moved I had been cut off from that luxury. I was also missing Olivia like crazy, and I think in an attempt to keep me happy my parents finally gave in and found some lessons that were affordable. They had noticed a small ad in the local newspaper at a place called Red Ribbon Stables that charged $15 a lesson. This was the most affordable place around, and it seemed just fine.

Red Ribbon Stables

ENTERING THE BARN FOR THE FIRST TIME I WAS nervous. Horses were completely new to me and the horse I would be riding seemed like a giant when I first laid eyes on him. I was taught how to brush my horse and I remember thinking how am I going to remember all of this? My coach was a tall blonde lady named Mary. Mary was very strong from doing most of the barn work herself. She was loud, friendly, firm, and when she talked she had a sparkle in her eye. Even so, to me she seemed rough. I was quite young and she scared me. I noticed that when she corrected the horses her tone of voice became very loud. It wasn't that she was mean, but she had a way about her that just wouldn't take no for an answer. Mary's confident way instilled confidence in the horses. For me it did something different. I couldn't say that I was scared or that I didn't think I could do it; I was more afraid of what she'd think of me if I failed. All I could do was try.

During the first lesson I was too nervous to do anything; I thought I might hurt the horse or the horse might step on me. During the second lesson, as I brushed my school horse, Sunny, who was tied in his stall, he pinned me up against the stall wall. He didn't squish me completely, but he put enough pressure on me so that I couldn't brush him or get away. Mary found me pinned there and told me how to move him over so he couldn't do that. Who knew he'd move over if you poked him with a bony finger in his belly? I was becoming more and more confident with the horses each time I rode, especially with knowing that the horse wouldn't be able to pin me against the wall whenever he felt like it. And so, after the second lesson I was completely hooked.

Over the next four years I was coached by Mary at Red Ribbon Stables. It was a small but competitive stable. I remember people coming up to me during shows and asking if certain horses were for sale. One time as I was watching Mary's daughter warm up for a class, five different individuals came and asked me if the horse was for sale, how much I'd take for her, and if she was off of the higher circuits. This was pretty exciting, as I felt like I myself owned the horse. The horse Mary's daughter was riding had actually been rescued from the St. Jacobs livestock exchange, which is pretty much a death trap for any horse who has gone lame or has injured a rider. The meat buyers take an average of 80% of the horses that come in each week. It's a sad place, but also a treasure trove for people who have an eye for the right horse. There have even been some race horses who have come out of there.

One March break on a Tuesday morning Mary brought all her students down to the auction. It was too cold to be riding, so she came up with this idea for a field trip instead. Red Ribbon Stables had their eye on a small pony who had actually been sold the night before, but we weren't aware of the sale and thought that he was going through on that day. Everyone was quite disappointed when he didn't go through the auction. Regardless, we still had a lot of fun there. There were horses we could easily imagine bringing home like big huge draft horses who had to duck to get into the auction ring. We saw lots of shaggy beasties, underfed horses, and ones who probably hadn't been dewormed or had their hooves trimmed their whole lives. Some of them had actually been bred to be sold here, just like a beef cow. One horse in particular gave us all a good laugh; he came in announcing himself the second the trailer had backed up to the loading docks. He was a stud and very friendly and good looking. His conformation was decent, actually excellent in comparison to the majority of the horses there. His only fault was that he couldn't bring his penis back up. The poor guy didn't seem to mind, but he kept kicking it around while he trotted around looking for a friend to pay attention to him. Mary chuckled and asked us how we'd like to take that into the show ring. She was joking around saying he'd make an excellent hunter for one of us. The things we remember. You'd think a sensitive soul like myself would remember the sad truth about what was happening at the auction rather than just the funny things. We always made light of the situation, but we understood what was happening. Even though we were young Mary had told us basically what was going on at the time. She would say things like, "You can't save them all", or "Who would you pick?" We would then discuss why the horse in question would or would not have been suitable. We used this sad place as a learning opportunity, or at least I did. Mary had a good eye and would tell us which horses looked like they were drugged. She showed us what to watch for. I learned about conformation, colours, and breeds. I learned what a healthy horse looks like, and of course what a sick or lame horse looks like.

Mary was a lot of fun as a coach, although I still couldn't say "no" to her. I enjoyed her lessons. This was what I looked forward to the whole week - even with my once a month emergency dis-mount (for those of you who don't speak horse yet, this means I fell off). There are a few falls in particular that really stood out. I can remember each fall like it was yesterday, where even the thought of them makes my heart race a little bit faster.

During the winter we mostly trail rode, as the ring would become icy. It was nice to get out in the open rather than ride around in circles. One time right after Christmas there had been a huge snow fall with nearly a foot and a half of snow. We headed out on the trail, just me and Mary this time, and we rode out for about an hour. I was on Indie, a large chestnut pony with a large white blaze on her face and a white spot on her belly. Indie was my favourite for a long time. She had attitude, but she was pretty. Mary was on her almost three-year-old draft/thoroughbred cross named Red; she was also a very pretty horse, although a lot taller than Indie. We came up to a huge tree that had fallen down in the storm. It had to be at least three feet tall. I was about 12 years old at this point so I could ride fairly well, but jumping was still a skill in the works.

My instructor said, "Well, we've come this far and we're not going to turn back - we'll have to jump it."

I said, "I don't think so; that's really high. Let's find a way around." But we couldn't find a way around, as the bush was too thick. So then I said, "Alright, you go first and I'll follow."

Mary said, "No, no, you go first so your horse won't try to catch up to mine."

Fine, fair reasoning. So I picked up a slow, reluctant trot, not wanting to go over it, and really not wanting to go fast over it. And Indie was a star! She jumped over the fallen tree straight out of the slow trot, landed, and even stopped after I fell onto her neck. Like I said, jumping was still in the works. So I shimmied back into the saddle and turned around. "Okay, your turn," I shouted to Mary.

Mary kind of laughed and said, "No way; I'm not jumping that!"

She reasoned that her horse was too young. Great, why hadn't I thought of that? So I was told to come on back over. I again tried to find another way around. The bush was really that thick. Finally, I decided to try the log again. I pushed Indie into a canter this time and she cleared it perfectly, landed in canter, and I stayed with her. The look on Mary's face was great, and it is something that will stick with me the rest of my life. When we got back to the barn Mary told everyone all about what her student had jumped and how well I'd done. She even told her daughter, who was a much better rider than me. Later when I was in my twenties I told her this story and she laughed it off saying she doesn't remember tricking me into jumping anything, but I'm sure she does.

On another trail ride we were on our way home. It was just Mary and myself again, on the same two mares. Almost directly across the road from Mary's barn was a very large alfalfa field belonging to a man named Hectare. I believe he had something close to a thousand acres and I thought his name was related to the amount of land he owned. I'm not so sure about that now, but the alfalfa field was definitely quite a few acres. Mary had asked if I wanted to canter, but I had said no as my balance at a gallop wasn't good. I knew my horse loved to gallop rather than canter in wide open spaces. So Mary said we'd just trot, and we started out side by side at a trot staying on the outside edges of the field to avoid damaging the crops. As I mentioned, Mary's horse was quite a bit bigger than mine. Indie, who was considered a pony, eventually had to canter to keep up with Red's long strides. I tried to hold her back and bring her down to a trot and Mary slowed her horse down a bit as well. Indie, however, felt she was being ripped off. Feeling she deserved to go for a nice gallop, she did just that. I lost my balance and ended up clinging to her neck, and then of course she picked up even more speed. Around the corner we stayed together with Mary shouting at me the whole time to sit up and pull her back. Every few strides I got my balance back enough to grab at the reins, but Indie wasn't having any of it; she eventually went into a full out dead run. At the second corner we had two options: go down a very narrow footpath towards the road which would lead to home, or turn right and continue around the field. I assumed Indie would take the path home as runaways often do, but I assumed very wrong. She swerved to the right at the last second and I came down underneath her. This has been my most serious fall to date. This is the kind of fall that makes people stop riding; it's the kind of fall that parents fear for their children to ever experience. Indie didn't mean to, but she kicked the back of my head and stepped square on my collarbone. I blacked out.

As a coach, taking riders outside is one thing, but not kids without established positions. That was a preventable accident. I was lucky I wasn't killed!!! I never told my parents all the details. They don't even remember hearing about the fall until years later.

When I became conscious I was in the field alone. I slowly tried to stand up and got to my knees before I saw Mary coming up the path leading Red. I asked her what had happened and was told, "Your horse just ran across the road; you'll have to go catch her now" very matter-of-factly. I needed to use Red to get my balance when I stood up, as things were still very blurry. I went down the footpath and found Indie in the neighbour's backyard. Indie, for her part, wasn't too concerned at all and she let me catch her. She stood still while I tried to get back on by myself. But I simply couldn't. Mary finally gave me a leg up and we walked home. Later my coach told my father I had taken a fall and that it wasn't a bad one. I went along with the story. I'm sure that at this point I still had so much adrenaline coursing through me that I really didn't feel very much at all. But a few days later I still could not stand up without seeing stars, and later I realized that this was definitely a concussion. I blacked out, so it was a head injury. My shoulder was painful but I didn't bother telling anyone that it hurt more than a bruise should. My goal was to show with Indie that following weekend, and I did. I was determined. I came in dead last and got a very pretty rainbow-coloured participant ribbon at the Touch N Go show, but I showed.

Looking at the positive side of this fall, I think that it taught me to be extra careful with my own students and to always advise my students and their parents to seek medical care after a bad fall or any fall involving the head. My parents still feel some anger towards Mary for not telling them the truth about the severity of my fall. Now as a coach I make sure to tell parents either in person if I see them or by text if I don't even if their child has just a simple fall where there seems to be no injury JUST IN CASE. There is a lot of pride that comes with horseback riding. As a parent you are worried that your child will be injured; as a child you want to prove to your parent that you are strong, smart, and safe. You most definitely do not want your parents pulling you out of your favourite sport because you were injured while doing it. So as a rider you take pride in your falls and your get-back-ons, and you ride through it. Riding isn't the safest but it's how we become tough. Riding is not a safe sport; it's one of the most dangerous sports there is. There is no sugar coating that.

In a way the determination that came out of this fall may have been what kept me riding. A lot of people who have taken that kind of fall have quit for a long time or stopped riding altogether.

But I didn't allow myself to feel scared; instead, I focused and pushed through. My parents didn't find out about the pain I was in until a few years later when I refused to go to swimming lessons because the front crawl made my shoulder hurt all over again. I still cannot swim the regular strokes for very long before I feel pain. I realize now that I was stupid to not have told anyone. My shoulder was finally looked at by doctors five years later, and I was told that it had healed just a bit off of where it should be.

I discovered many things while riding with Mary. One discovery was that I am very allergic to cigarette smoke. We had gone on a big group trail ride with five or six of us. I was right behind Mary and was riding a Thoroughbred gelding named Midnight. It was nearing Christmas time again and we were all singing Christmas carols. All the fluffy horses puffing out silver mist from their nostrils and picking up their feet extra high through the deep snowy trail made a very beautiful sight. We were riding along a river that was frozen in sparkling circles and icicles. Mary, however, was a smoker, and as I was singing along I inhaled a puff of smoke that had me coughing until I fainted. Fainting is never a good thing to happen on a Thoroughbred. Thoroughbreds are a breed that is known for speed; they are bred to race. This particular horse was a bit older but he had been on the track at some point and he seemed to feel the need to gallop the second I went limp. This is, of course, what the people riding behind me reported. I remember getting untangled from the stirrup while hanging completely upside down. Luckily, the horse was quite tall and my head hadn't hit the ground or his hooves while he was running.

It's amazing the luck that I have. Most people go through their lives with only half this luck. I do not go looking for these adventures; I merely end up in them. Of course I love an adrenaline rush the same as the next person, but my nature is quiet, shy, and laid back for the most part. In general these little adventures just seem to find me on their own.

Mary was a great coach and I learned a lot from her. She would let me try everything.

"You want to ride bareback? Fine, but you have to get on by yourself with no mounting block."

I once got to lunge Red, though I wasn't very good since it was my first time. Red decided she was a pro jumper and leaped over some jumps that had been left up in the ring. I got in trouble for that. Mary was the one who really got me into the teaching and coaching idea, that is of course after I grew too tall to become a jockey and my racing dreams were squashed. I learned a lot from her about both good and bad ways of handling situations, and it's that same concept that I have taken with me to future stables. Learn everything you can. Take the good stuff with you and leave anything that you don't need behind, but still learn it. With horse riding you really can't learn too much. There are of course a million and one ways to do something, and every horse trainer will tell you that their way is the right and only way. That's just the horse business. I've met coaches who have gotten by on pure confidence, but absolutely no ability at all. If you believe it, people believe you, and you develop a following. The second you doubt yourself, people start doubting you. But I don't agree with that. If you're cocky and bold to the point where everyone assumes you're right, then what are they really going to learn from you, other than to be cocky? As a real trainer you eventually need to find your own middle ground and actually develop methods that work for you. Once you've established this, then you need to find people who believe in it as well and even further, will pay you.

When I left Red Ribbon Stables, I was upset. I had shown up with my dad for a riding lesson and I'd found the horses loose out of their pens, stalls not done, the aisles filthy, and the tack thrown everywhere. The place looked like it had been robbed, almost as if someone had gone through everything in a hurry. After not finding my instructor or any members of her family, we got fed up and I decided I would leave. My dad didn't try to persuade me in either direction; he just calmly drove. Halfway home I asked if we could turn around and get my chaps and brushes I'd left there, as I didn't intend on going back. We went back, I got my stuff, and then we went home. A few weeks later Mary came to our door to say goodbye to me. She said that she was sad to see me go and she started crying. To me this was heart-wrenching. I didn't know that such a strong woman could feel pain, and at something so small as having a student leave. Mary and I kept in touch for a few years after that and I came out and trail rode on the rare occasion just to visit and see the horses again. Mary moved away about two years later. We didn't know where she had gone. I tried to track her down, but never seemed to be able to find her. I'd even look up show results to see if she was still in the horse business, but I couldn't find her. It was nearly 10 years before we by chance reconnected.

Willow Creek Stables

WHEN I STARTED AT WILLOW CREEK STABLES I WAS shocked. I had gone from being one of the top riders at the barn to being a rider who literally couldn't steer or stop a horse. These horses were trained differently; they responded completely opposite of what I was used to. I started out riding whoever was available. Occasionally I would ride a silly old Arabian gelding, Shadow was his name, and he spooked around every corner and at every shadow. He was slow and bouncy, but a babysitter as well. He took good care of the students who were nervous, as even when he spooked he made sure they were still there. He didn't leave anyone in mid-air. Secret was another horse I came to like. She was an older Appendix Quarter Horse mare, a plain looking chestnut with a white stripe on her face. She was a bit bratty and had a mind of her own, but she was also simple to ride. She liked to get the lessons over with so she'd go along with almost anything. The horse I really clicked with at Willow Creek was a retired eventer who went by the name of Elvis. He was black with a perfect white star. Probably close to 16 hands high (which is fairly big for a lesson horse), he had a sway back that made him look closer to only 15 hands. Elvis was a blast, even though my first lessons consisted of not being able to stop. He was strong and would pull you right out of the saddle regardless of how far down your heels were.

One day the instructor, Beatrice, took us out on their cross country course. After coming to this new stable I had completely lost all confidence. Being on horses who simply didn't listen to anything I had been previously taught and having a new instructor who was gruff to say the least would also do that to me. Beatrice asked the group to go over a small "table" jump, which is basically three steps with the middle one being the highest. I was nervous and I held back to the end. Elvis, however, was an old pro at this and didn't like having to wait his turn. When it was our turn I asked for a trot and got a canter. Going up and over to the other side he took off at a dead run and finished most of the course. Oddly enough I stayed on this time. Needless to say, my horse connections on the Internet had taught me how to do an emergency stop and so shortly after that incident Elvis and I started getting along much better. But overall at Beatrice's stable I did not progress, and the other students did not treat me with any respect. Beatrice was not a good coach for me and I left after only a year.

Moving On Again

I WAS 14 NOW AND HAD DECIDED TO CHANGE STABLES once again. I had become a true internet addict and had studied each stable within a half hour radius of our house. There were about four to choose from and I choose CLC. They had a simple easy-to-use website that had a little blurb about each of their horses. The only thing that worried me was the fact that most of their horses were quite old. CLC stood for all sorts of things: Caliv and Laura Cantell, the owners of the property; Classic Lane Candy, the adorable older pony who had taught at least a thousand different people how to ride; as well as another reason that has slipped my mind, which of course is probably the real meaning of the acronym. I was given a full tour of the property by the barn owner himself who was a very kind older gentle-man with the nicest eyes and the kindest way of talking you will ever find. He was meant to be a professional hockey player but when his hockey days were over he had found a great passion for horses. Caliv had a way about him that never made you feel out of place and he made sure that everyone was happy. He ran this successful riding stable which had an indoor arena with a heated viewing lounge. My parents were quickly hooked on that comfortable fact. I was hooked fast too, but then again I was a teenager who loved horses. There was one horse in particular that I was attracted to. From a distance she looked just like Sandy, one of Mary's horses who was a full sister to Red and only a year younger. Up close she wasn't Sandy at all, but since I had shown an interest I was placed on Sierra for my riding lessons. This was after a full evaluation of my riding skills on the flat and over fences by one of the coaches using a bombproof older school horse. I told you they were good.

Sierra was huge at 16.2 hands and her size was mostly a result of draft breeding. However, she had something else bred into her and that something else made her much too much horse for me. During our second lesson together I could not get her to stop cantering; eventually she picked up speed and I lost my balance. The instructor yelled at everyone to stop and stand in the middle, but Sierra kept running. After about four laps I finally grabbed the outside rein and reined her tight to the fence until she stopped. Soon after I was switched to a quieter more forgiving horse. My coach was brilliant. She instantly became my role model, and she still is. I think her biggest strength is not in the horse training nor in the coaching, although her skills in these areas are absolutely nothing to laugh at. But I think her true ability lay in her way of reading her riders. She knew when it was a good time to push and she knew when we were starting to hit our limit. In those moments she would always take away the pressure by making the exercise easier or by taking a break from it all together right before we hit that dead end wall. She read the horses just as well. If they were getting frustrated with the exercise or with their rider, guaranteed Steph would know before the rider did. Oh, did I mention her name was Steph, just like me?

In our lesson we had between five and seven riders. My name was switched to Stephi to make things a little bit easier. Another girl in the class who was a year older than myself was also a Steph, but we generally called her Stephanie. I think there were eight Stephs at the stable in total, including the owner's daughter. It was often very confusing.

During Steph's lessons I learned a lot, and with a large group of riders who were at my level or slightly above I progressed and pushed myself a lot harder. Steph would insist that we do other physical activities outside of riding to stay fit, and even quizzed us on what we had done that week. Riding with Steph was a highlight of my teen years. I worked hard to progress further each week. If I had to miss a riding lesson it was okay, because then I would get a make-up private lesson - which meant far more intense training.

Outside of riding I went through a lot of struggles in my teens. I had a few months where I ate almost nothing because I wanted to lose weight. My self-confidence was at its worst and I probably said a total of 80 words throughout my high school years. I didn't have very many friends and I never felt that I was accepted in school. I know that a lot of people may feel that school isn't actually the best time of your life that some people might say it is. Believe me; it gets better. The growing, the learning, and the fun don't have to end with high school or even post-secondary school - not if you don't want it to. I continue to learn and to grow each day.

Boys

BOYS, LET'S TALK ABOUT BOYS. IT'S SO MUCH EASIER for me to tell you about horses and adventures than it is to talk about my love life in a book that could be read by my students, my clients, and a whole whack of strangers I may never meet who will no doubt judge me. I have had lots of boyfriends - nothing serious, but all through public school and high school I was dating on and off. My first "boyfriend" was a very cute kid named Adam. We were in the same grade, and we were definitely the first in our class to date. After a couple of months he cheated on me and started dating Danielle, however cheated is used very lightly as the most any of the grade threes would do was hold hands or dance. Regardless, I was still sad and I remember my mom trying to console me.

At public school I was constantly bullied. I went to counseling occasionally with a favourite teacher, though I was soon dropped because I didn't have any "real" problems. I was chronically shy to the point where I hated myself for my lack of confidence. I had a lot going on in my mind but I didn't know how to put my thoughts into words and talk about it. When children's parents were getting divorced and other problems were showing up in the school system, those were the kids who got the counseling - not the child with low self-esteem. But to other kids the one with low self-esteem is an easy target.

MSN Messenger was very popular at that time. Most of the kids in my class were on it in the evenings, myself included. One day I got a request to add an email: Benderomed@hotmail.com. I was asked if I wished to add this person to my contact list. Yes sure; it's probably the Ben from my class. Ben it was. He chatted a bit with me, then a few days later informed me he was in love with me and wanted to date. He asked if I would go out with him. I hesitated because Ben was a large or even what might be considered an obese boy. Plus he never really talked to me in class. He was never mean, but he didn't show that he wanted to be friends either. I hesitated because of his size; I judged him because of how he looked. Instead of rejecting him I first asked: "What makes you want to date me?"

He replied: "I always have, I was just too shy to ask you."

That got through to me. I agreed, and we mutually became a couple online. The next day at school as I walked across the tarmac I could hear people gossiping. I could see them staring at me and I could hear some of them giggling. I assumed they were shocked I was dating Ben, and that he had probably told someone who had told everyone. I ignored them and let them think what they wanted. A couple of minutes went by and Keith approached me. Keith was Ben's close friend, as well as the older brother of one of my close friends. Keith had another friend with him, though I cannot recall his name - perhaps he was a Kyle or a Bret. Keith snickered and gave me a rude comment about how gross Ben was.

"Why would you want to date him?" he questioned.

Ben was standing against the wall looking extremely embarrassed about the whole thing.

I stuck to my guns and said, "He's nice. I like him."

I glared straight back at Keith and walked away. Before long it was first recess and Keith and his friends were at it again, asking me why. Finally I said that Ben had asked me to be his girlfriend online. That got them going, and then the truth came out. It hadn't been Ben chatting with me online. Someone had created an account to look like it belonged to Ben and had asked me out to publicly humiliate me, or perhaps to publicly humiliate Ben. Whatever their motives had been, they had succeeded in making both of us feel horrible.

After a couple of days I approached Ben. I said that I was sorry, and that if he had actually asked me out I would have said yes. I said that I hadn't known it wasn't him. But he didn't want to talk to me.

A couple of days later I was preparing to head home for lunch, and as I was leaving the building Keith and his friends were at the doors.

They shouted "Why are you going home? Don't you like it here? Don't you want to be with Ben? Why aren't you staying here for lunch?"

I tried to push past them and ignore them without responding. They wouldn't have it; they grabbed me. They pushed me back against a wall and continued yelling their insults at me. I hit Keith as hard as I could across the face, yelled "Let go of me!" and walked out. I didn't run out because I didn't want to show fear. I just walked away without turning back. When I got up past the top of the hill I broke into a run and got home as fast as I could. I cried. The tears had started when I started running and they didn't stop once I got home. I cried for what felt like an eternity. My parents were both at work and my brothers had stayed for lunch at school. Alone, I got myself together and went back in time for the second half of the day. No one said a word to me; in fact hardly anyone spoke to me for the rest of the school year.

Since then I've had a hard time letting anyone get too close or letting any relationship become too serious. I am scared to. Sometimes I joke and say I'm scared of "commitment", just because that phrase seems to be the only generalization that is acceptable these days. Each week there was only one thing I looked forward to: my riding lesson. I wasn't very good at riding yet, and I knew that, but I wanted to become a great rider. This goal drove me forward with a stronger passion than I had ever felt before. I enjoyed the barn chores, and simply being around the horses of course, but I really loved to ride.

My first high school was a Catholic high school, and though I'm not Catholic, I got along there fine. We wore uniforms and had access to state-of-the-art facilities. There were three floors to the school, as well as portables for all of the classes that couldn't be accommodated indoors. My parents insisted I take a music course, and I learned to play the trumpet. I enjoyed it so much I even joined an after school jazz band. As a bonus each day I was still able to walk home for lunch since the school was just up the road from our house.

When I had graduated from elementary school I had two choices of where to go for high school. The other high school was a humongous old building that looked just like a castle. It was a public school. That meant no uniforms and no religious prayers, but an excellent variety of extracurricular activities available. Though I would have had to take a bus to the other end of the city, the majority of my class was going there so at least I wouldn't have felt like a new student. However, this school had its share of stories. Most were stories about it being haunted from when the school had been a boys' boarding school. And there were stories of the school going through a transition period when the principal was forced to accept female students but had refused and left with most of the staff. The tale that made my choice of schools clear to me still gives me shivers. This particular story was a bit more modern from a couple years after the school had been turned from a boarding school into an secondary school. Feel free to skip this next part if you go to a high school that resembles a large castle.

I will try to tell this true story, exactly the way it was told to me.

Cambridge is the city of ghosts with some of the oldest buildings in Ontario and one of the oldest schools in all of Canada. Three students - two boys and one girl - had just started their grade nine year at the school. It was the first week of classes, and on Thursday, after class was over, parents were invited to have a tour of the school and to meet their children's teachers. The three friends met up. Bored with their parents, they asked to go off together on their own. The parents were busy looking at art work and barely noticed that their kids had left. The three wandered the halls aimlessly, not really all that excited to be back at school. One of the boys suggested they check out the third floor. The third floor was off limits as it was still being converted from dorms to classrooms. The other two agreed that it would at least be interesting. They tried all the doors in each wing to access the third floor staircase, but all of the doors were locked. Finally, just as they were about to give up and find their parents again, they tried a big wooden door. This was the only wooden door remaining, as all the other doors had been converted to steel.

Though they'd already tried the wooden door with no success, this time it opened. The door opened easily with a slight squeak. The students glanced at each other, and trying to act brave they shrugged and ventured up the stairs. The top floor wasn't very exciting at all, as each room was just like the floor below with chalkboards and emptiness. Realizing there wasn't anything exciting to do on the third floor they returned down the stairs and back to the second floor, only to find that the large wooden door was once again locked.

The young girl was starting to panic, and she banged against the door and yelled for someone to come open it. The boys decided there was a chance another door would be unlocked so together they tried every stairwell only to arrive at steel doors that were locked from both sides. They sprinted back up the stairs to the third floor and ran to the end of the hall where there was a large window. Outside it was starting to get dark as the last few cars were leaving the parking lot. One of the boys swore under his breath. They eventually decided to give up. They chose a classroom close to the big wooden door and curled up together with their jackets covering their legs to keep warm.

In the middle of the night the young girl woke up to find that both of her friends had disappeared. She panicked and ran down the hall yelling for them, checking each and every room. She then ran down each stairwell and tried each door. She even kicked the big wooden door, but it wouldn't budge. She ran back to the classroom they had slept in. No one was there, but she could see clearly written on the chalkboard in huge red letters the words "get out". The red was not written in chalk. Completely panic-stricken she tried the wooden door again, clawing at the door as hard as she could, but it remained shut. She ran down the main hall and she kept running, eventually crashing through the window and falling down three floors to the hard ground beneath. She died on impact. At school on Friday when the boys showed up for class they were met by police and questioned. As well as the young girl's body on the ground below the broken window, investigators had found fingernails stuck in the back of the wooden door. When the boys found out they told the police exactly what had happened. They explained how the three of them had been exploring and had become locked up on the third floor. They then stated that they had found a way out in the middle of the night, as one of the doors previously locked had finally opened. They'd left their friend there as a trick, and had planned to come back for her in the morning. They had never written on the chalkboard.

Anyways, let's get back to the boys...

In high school it was the musicians: a drummer, a bass player, and a trumpeter. They were always laughing and having fun so I was attracted to them the most. Again, it was nothing serious - the longest a boyfriend would last would be a month or two. We may have kissed, may not have; it wasn't really important. It was more about just having someone that was yours and experiencing the whole dating and love thing. Most of the time we took it seriously but looking back I realize that no one was serious about it at all. None of us thought about marriage or sex or kids. Okay maybe sex but definitely not the other two.

My parents and I struggled a lot with what was allowed and what wasn't. I wasn't a bad child by any means. I didn't drink or smoke, but I wanted more freedom. Having to be in the house before dark, having to ask before I could have a friend over, and having to make sure it was okay before nearly everything I did made my opinion of my parents very low. I felt that if I was a responsible kid and I wasn't getting into trouble, then why couldn't they just let me have free rein? I would have settled with a looser rein, but I didn't get it. My parents stuck to their guns and continued to do so until I left for college. My high school years were hell. I took my anger out on my mom a lot; I knew I was doing it too. I did it because I was frustrated. It wasn't that I didn't love her, but I was angry, and I knew that my mom was the only one around strong enough to take it out on. Most teenagers go through this phase with their moms. There are no words to describe how hard it is to handle your emotions. They bottle up inside you, especially when you are quiet and shy in public, particularly at school, and then when you come home a simple rule or a question just makes you lose it. I am thankful I had a supportive mother who helped me through these times. Now she is like a best friend. I talk to her more often than I do my best friends, and we visit as often as we can.

I struggled through these years - not just because of my parents' tight rein, but also because of my friends. I didn't have anyone who was very close to me. I had a few friends who I could hang out with but no one who liked horses in the same way and no one who went out of their way to hang out with me. I did not do well in school but I wasn't really concerned. I would daydream, stare out the window, and imagine jumping over the light posts or the fences around the running track. I would spend easily half of class doodling horses across margins and the bottom of paragraphs when I had stopped taking notes. I felt like the only world I really fit into was the horse world. I couldn't understand why all people did not have this strong of a passion. Even if it wasn't for horses, I felt that everyone should be passionate about something they loved.

I had a friend. He was quiet and we met in our very first class of high school when we had to partner up for an icebreaker exercise. Matt was a boy who was up for anything and really didn't care what. He had four older sisters, so going home didn't appeal to him for the most part. One afternoon we headed off to the conservation area. We were in the same gym class and we felt humiliated about not participating with the same amount of integrity as the other students. So we figured that walking around the lake would be more exercise than class. I took my mom's cell phone and told her we were going for a walk around the block. Since we needed to be home before dark, I couldn't say we were going to the conservation area as she would have put a stop to that right then and there.

Once we arrived we found that the trail around the lake only went about 30 feet before it became thick bush that hadn't ever been walked. We were up for this adventure though and so we kept going. We had thought to bring drinks along and drank our orange juice halfway through. After about two hours we came to a clearing where there was a large grassy section and a large number of Canadian geese. This was kind of funny, we thought, and we decided to change direction and walk up a grassy hill a ways. It turned out that this hill came to a paved road. Now we were highly amused: why would there be a nicely paved road in the middle of nowhere? So we did eenie, meenie, miney, mo and chose a direction to follow. After about 15 more minutes of walking we came to a large parking lot in front of a very impressive dark glass building. This looked like a medical centre of some sort, and we were intrigued. At the other end of the parking lot we found a sign that read Cambridge Rehabilitation Centre, This Way (with an arrow), No Trespassing Permitted. So Matt and I, two high school students, now knew the location of the secret rehab centre where all the celebrities go when they're caught. "No trespassing", however, put a damper on things. We imagined they were after us so we kept following the paved road and eventually ended up on Clyde Road (now they'll really be mad at me for blowing their location!). The sign at the end of the driveway said nothing about rehabilitation, only something about the conservation area that we had been in. There was still a bit of light outside and we weren't particularly tired, so we kept walking. I knew the road because this was where Red Ribbon Stables used to be. We were quite a ways further down from the stable, but I thought it would be fun to walk there. Matt of course went along with it; he was up for anything.

We came to the top of a very large hill and saw a sign that advertised horse boarding. I was still dreaming of owning my own horse, so I figured it would be great to go check this place out. The owner was rude and only grudgingly showed us around. I had convinced him that my father was very wealthy and was buying me a horse and that I was going to be deciding where to keep it. I didn't know it, but I was a pretty great liar back then. We left after asking when a good time to bring my father would be. The owner suggested the upcoming weekend. I was excited as the board wasn't as high as CLC's and this stable was a lot closer. Actually, it was exactly a two-and-a-half hour walk, which we found out as we walked home taking the main roads this time. My mother was hysterical when I told her where we had gone, but it was worth it.

Cricket

THE NEXT WEEKEND I HAD SOMEHOW CONVINCED MY dad to take me back there. Again, as I am a very lucky person, it was only natural that we met a lady named Annetta on that day. She had a beautiful large black horse and after I was suckered into leading him around for her two little girls to ride (while she held them up there), she asked if I would like to co-board Billy. For $80 a month I got to ride twice a week and do his stall on the days I came out. Extra riding time outside of my weekly lesson at CLC was great. To me, this arrangement was perfect; to my parents, it seemed like a rip-off.

I soon discovered that Billy was very good at nothing. He was basically right off the track but had been a pet and done trails for a few years. He was stiff as a board; he did not bend left or right. He also did not trot or canter; instead, he did pace which he typically used to unseat me. He knew what whoa meant, and he knew what go meant - well sort of. After a year I had him doing a walk and a trot and a little bit of bending in each direction. He would also start cantering on our trail rides. He would often switch his trot back to a pace and I would growl "Bill!" in my lowest meanest voice and then he would switch, or else he'd have to walk again and pick up a trot for me. I learned a lot with Billy, as he taught me how to actually ride. I say this with the greatest respect to my instructors of course. Riding a horse like Billy will teach you to "stick". I do not have a real natural Velcro butt like a lot of great riders, but Billy helped me develop one. Riding at this stable was a great experience for me. I was constantly being yelled at by other boarders but I also made a lot of friends.

One of my very favourite boarders was a cowboy named Randy who owned two horses: Rain and Buck. He rode Buck mainly, a small Buckskin Quarter Horse. Randy and Buck rarely missed a day on the trails. Randy was well over 80 years old when I met him, and was still riding daily. He passed away in March 2008 and is very much missed. Everyone who met Randy loved him. He was always extremely friendly and had a pet name for everyone. I was Squeak, short for Pip Squeak. One of his favourite things to do was to tell stories. I have no idea if half of the stories he told were true. After hearing them so often, as he did repeat them often, they became some of my favourite stories as well. For instance, when Randy was in his mid-teens he lived with his family at a large ranch where his father bred horses. One night when Randy went out with his brother, his brother drank quite a bit and became very drunk. When they got home his brother hopped on his father's prized horse, a beautiful great big albino stallion.

He laughed and said, "Hey Randy, open up the gate there."

Randy did, and his brother, riding bareback, rode the horse out into the yard and right up onto the porch of their big farm house.

"Hey Randy, why don't you open up the door?"

Randy laughed, thinking his brother was not really going to ride the horse inside, and opened the door. Randy's brother marched the horse right through the door and up the grand staircase to the second floor where he dismounted, with grace of course, and walked a few steps to his bedroom to sleep for the night. In the morning their father woke up to find his beautiful stallion waiting patiently at the top of the staircase. They spent the whole morning trying to get the horse back down.

Randy was one of the best cowboys you could ever find. He was very polite. He joked around all the time but always kept his tongue when the parents were around. He'd often give me pointers on my training with Billy. When he saw my riding improve, he eventually allowed me to ride Buck, but only in fenced-in areas. He'd ask me to ride Buck in from the field so that he wouldn't have to walk out, and he taught me how to do the basic barrel racing pattern. Though at first he had me ride in his big old Western saddle, I slipped around so much that I opted to ride bareback from then on. Buck and I fit together quite well. There are some horses you just seem to be able to sit with and ride without effort. I didn't meet another horse like him until much later when I found Atlas (more about him later). I would choose to ride Buck over any other boarder's horse that was available to me.

After the first year, a lot of the boarders were allowing me to ride their horses to keep them energized during the week. I was becoming quite fit. During the spring, summer, and fall I'd bike the 45-minute ride to the barn, clean Billy's stall, clean Beauty's stall, and then clean whoever else's needed to be done. After that I'd ride. There was usually a small group that would go for a trail ride and afterwards I would work Billy in the ring on transitions or over poles. Beauty was Annetta's best friend's little pony. She was 25 years old and she was still full of spunk. Eventually I met the daughter of Annetta's best friend - her name was Jacqueline. Jacqueline is about four years younger than me but we became very close from the first day we met. Me and Jacqueline ended up best friends for seven years before we gradually drifted our separate ways. We rode together at least three times a week, even in the winter. Soon Jacqueline started riding in my lessons at CLC as well. When Beauty was 26 we taught her how to jump. This little horse was such a star that we took her and Billy to the schooling shows at Touch N Go. Beauty with Jacqueline riding cleaned up. Out of classes with 20 competitors Jacqueline would get fourth and fifth place with a 26-year-old horse who had just learned to jump - it was remarkable. Beauty retired soon after when her back wasn't strong enough for daily riding, but she enjoyed every moment she had as Jacqueline's show partner.

After a year of co-boarding Billy, I had become fairly close to most of the boarders at the stable. I knew the ins and outs of when the crabby ladies would be around and that sort of thing. I definitely knew how to turn off the lights in the main barn and did it on a regular basis without being asked. The old ladies used to try and pin the lights on us.

One day I found out that a lady named Harriet had bought a new horse. She already had a little Appaloosa filly at the barn. Her new horse was to come home on a Tuesday. That Tuesday was my day to ride Billy, so I peddled out to the barn and saw a very pretty horse's face hanging out the barn door. The moment he saw me he took off into the barnyard. I came in and ran into the barn manager first. He warned me very sternly that this horse was new and seemed crazy, and so I wasn't to touch him. The second he was out of sight I touched the new horse. He was shy and he had a very wild look in his eyes. Every few minutes he'd take off with his tail flailing behind him and run the fence line where the other horses were watching calmly. He didn't seem to mind me, and so I would run my hands up and down his neck while he munched on grass in the rare moments when he wasn't trotting the fence at full speed. Harriet came later that evening after I had ridden Billy, and she told me a little bit about him. He was off the race track and he was only two; she was going to train him and ride him since he was older than her other horse. I thought he was absolutely gorgeous. Within a couple of weeks I had Harriet convinced to let me train Cricket. I had to pay $35 a month to work with him. At this point that was fine; this would be good experience and it would be with a horse I had fallen in love with literally at first sight. Two months went by and Harriet went bankrupt. She had to sell Cricket. She wanted $1200 for him with a huge western saddle and bridle, or $900 for just him. I begged and begged my parents but they weren't interested at all.

I finally put together a business plan and decided to ask my grandfather if he would go into business with me, fifty/fifty. We'd split all costs, train him, and sell him for much more once he was trained. When my grandparents took me and my brothers to a children's museum, I approached my grandmother and asked if she thought Grandpa would be interested in such an idea. She made a bit of a face like she'd eaten something sour and said I'd just have to ask him myself.

My grandfather is my hero, because he helped me buy my best friend, my first pony. We paid $800 for him and I was the happiest person on earth. I babysat as much as I could, I dog-walked, I did my own paper route, and I helped both my brothers with theirs. I had to stop co-boarding Billy because boarding cost much more money than co-boarding, but Annetta was very sweet and let me ride Billy a few times a week if I did his stall when I was out there. So I continued to train Billy while I was starting to train my own first horse. Harriet had been able to back him twice (sit on his back). I had heard through the other boarders that he had tried very hard to buck her off but because she weighed nearly as much as he did, he simply couldn't get off the ground. It was true that Harriet was heavy, but it was more so that Cricket was very small. I remember my second time on him. I rode him bareback with my dad at his head and I could touch my toes right underneath his belly. His name came from the racetrack since he was the smallest horse there. Cricket is shown under the name Spazzmatic The Wonder Pony. The judges get a kick out of that name, but it really suits him.

For $25 a very nice young boarder sold me her English saddle with stirrups, a saddle pad, and a girth. It of course did not fit and I rode in it only twice before I sold it. On consignment it sold for $125, and I put that money towards another saddle. The only one I could afford was a pony saddle. It was much too small for my teenager butt, but it fit Cricket quite well. For my birthday later that year I was given money from my parents which I put towards a brand new HDR saddle, and so I finally had a saddle that fit us both. I love to trade up saddles. Even now I head down to the St. Jacobs auction and pick out an old ugly saddle. Typically it's full of cobwebs and hasn't been used in ages. With the tricks that Randy taught me about leather care, I can usually restore it to a nice supple leather with a decent shine and sell it for a few times more than what I paid for it.

Cricket is a very sensitive horse. He connected with me even though I was still a bit timid with training. I was firm and consistent, and he responded by trusting me. We became quite a team. The first two rides were on the lead-line with my dad or Jacqueline leading Cricket. After the initial few rides to make sure he didn't want to buck me off, we started riding in a grass ring beside the barn. In our first training sessions Cricket did very well. He learned to stop, go, and steer in both directions at a walk and trot. However, we did have one issue those first few sessions. Cricket decided he rather liked the gate, probably because I'd stop there to chat with whoever was around watching me. At about our fourth or fifth ride he stopped at the gate and refused to move. The first time he tried it, I convinced him to go forward again and figured we were in the clear. On the next lap, however, he skidded himself right over to the corner by the gate and planted his feet. After about five minutes of trying to get him to move in any direction, I was fed up and got off. I walked into the tack room and left him there in the ring alone, completely tacked up and unsupervised (not the smartest thing I've done but surely not the worst). I grabbed Annetta's spurs from her tack trunk and took my time putting them on. I had never before worn spurs and I wasn't proud of myself for putting them on, but I was frustrated enough to try it. Just like I suspected, Cricket still hadn't budged. He seemed a bit curious about what I was doing until I hopped back on and he went right back to having cement feet. So I asked him nicely.

With my voice and a soft leg I said, "Cricket, walk on."

Cricket stood there and kind of glanced at me as if to shrug and say, "Yeah right, that worked last time."

Then I turned in my heels and gave him a nudge. Poor Cricket's head shot straight up in the air; this time he glanced back with a confused look.

I simply said aloud, "Cricket, walk on." Cricket walked on.

My Cricket is one of the smartest horses in the world. He remembers everything he is taught, and he knows the difference between a child, a beginner, a snob, and a decent rider. A great trainer I know once told me he absolutely hates smart horses. He'd say this right to a horse's owner if they claimed their horse was "smart". I don't mind smart horses. They won't make you money in a hurry if your job is to train them, but they will be the best horse to work with once they are trained.

When our second week of riding came around, Cricket was considered green broke. He knew what whoa meant and he knew the general basics at a walk and trot. Cowboy Randy decided we should go on a trail ride. For Cricket's first trail ride, rather than staying on the property which had a few hundred acres of nicely groomed trails to ride on, Randy chose the conservation area. Getting to the conservation area was great fun. First we crossed a busy country road, and then we went over a steel bridge that was set a hundred feet above the train tracks. Why this was the trail of choice is beyond me now. While attempting to cross the road I discovered Cricket was terrified of the yellow line. You know that bright yellow line that splits the traffic on busy roads? He stopped, flared his nostrils, glared at it, then spooked and tried to run home. He'd get a few steps in before I'd turn him back around to face it and ask him to go over it again. After a minute of this there were cars lining up on both sides of us and they were getting impatient.

Randy said in the calmest voice ever: "Just turn him around. Alright, now back him up."

Cricket backed up a few steps and was halfway over the line. Once he was that far he wasn't concerned and he turned around and walked across without a problem. This is one of the neatest tricks I've ever seen work. From then on Cricket wasn't afraid of the yellow line, and he trusted me more and more each ride. Cowboy Randy earned my respect that day. I've remembered this trick for sure. My pony was a star for the rest of the ride; he even went over the bridge without a problem (as long as his chest was at Buck's butt the entire time). Don't look down Cricket boy, it's scary, keep those eyes up! This bridge was scary: 100 feet above the ground and louder than any wooden bridge. There was a railing on each side but it only came to about my ankle level. If a horse were to jump sideways, you could potentially fall a very long ways. Heaven forbid there be a train, although if you weren't dead after that fall you may be praying for a train to hit you anyway.

I kept Cricket there for only two months. Within those two months we became very close. He learned how to jump and basic dressage movements, and we even headed out to a few local shows. He learned a few tricks as well. I taught him to catch a kiss. If I blew it to him from across the barn, he'd act like he just got punched in the nose. He caught my kisses quite well. He also perfected a bow. Admittedly he will literally do anything for a candy cane, so I really can't take much credit for his trick training. I, however, learned a lot. I learned not to jump a horse who isn't mature, whether it be emotionally or physically. I learned that the piaffe is a lot harder to do than it looks, and I learned that plastic bags in trees are better left alone. We had an awful fall together when I asked Cricket to go closer to a plastic bag in a tree and he spun around to bolt and lost his footing. While we were going down I could see his right hind leg beside me. He tore a large muscle near his hip and scared himself half to death. He had come down on my leg, but since he was so light I was only bruised. He was very sore though, and I had to spend a few months conditioning him before I could ride him again. This was my first little lesson which should have taught me to choose my battles carefully. Over the next few years this same lesson was repeated and I hope that now I've finally learned it. Basically, if you don't think you'll win or that your horse will understand within a short amount of time, it probably isn't a battle worth fighting - at least not that day. Horses learn best in short sweet sessions. Break the problem up into smaller questions, and then they'll learn it.

I also learned a lot about how to manage a barn, or how not to. Learning from mistakes other people make is still learning. Cricket coliced twice because of improper management. Of course, not all colic is preventable, but these two incidents could have been caught before they got worse. A horse that typically drinks its water, eats all its grain, and finishes every last bit of hay is an easy horse to monitor. Cricket was, and still is, one of these horses. Twice I came to the barn to find his water bucket full, his hay untouched, and bits of grain left in his bin. I'd find Cricket in the field sulking or laying down looking asleep, but obviously in a great deal of pain.

From here we moved to another boarding stable called Spooky Ridge Stables. This was a small boarding barn, but they kept tabs on everything. The barn owner, Jenna, was incredibly organized, and she always looked out for the horses' best interests.

Cricket and I were excited to attend CLC's dressage show. I spent the previous day pulling his mane, bathing him, and then braiding him. I turned him out for a few hours so that he could eat grass while I polished our tack, and then I went to grab him and bring him in early so that he wouldn't roll in the mud. He wasn't pleased about coming in again after all that fuss, and so he ignored me by walking away and occasionally trotting away from me. Finally I got smart and put the lead rope over his neck so I that could hold him to catch him. He had his head down trying to eat and was doing his absolute best to ignore me. When the chain of the lead rope hit the ground, he spooked and spun backwards. His head came up and his forehead made contact with my nose. He then let me catch him and I brought him back to the barn. Jenna was busy talking to one of the other boarders while I stood there bleeding, trying to interrupt politely. I needed assistance. Too polite for my own good, they eventually noticed me and instantly stopped talking to help me.

My nose was likely broken, but at the show the next day I was supposed to be doing a costume class dressed up as Barbie. That felt too ironic.

The next day I woke up and put on more makeup than I'd ever worn in my life to cover the bruising under my eyes. I pulled it off and we even took home a first place for that class.

Returning to Spooky Ridge Stables after the show we found Harriet waiting for us. She was in the parking lot with an empty horse trailer hooked onto her vehicle. Confused, I unloaded Cricket and put him in his stall. Jenna seemed flustered and explained to me quietly that she was going to tell Harriet to leave as she had no business here. I clued in that Harriet was hanging around waiting for us. She wasn't planning on picking up any other horse except for my horse. She had sold him to me fair and square a few months before, but once she had come out of bankruptcy she had thought she could just come and pick up the horse. This is one of the many stories I will tell you about crazy horse people. Jenna firmly told her to leave, and that was that. I still worry when I see Harriet. I saw her a few years later at a Standardbred Series horse show and I stayed put in my saddle on my horse for the entire day. What would have happened if we hadn't gone to the show that day, or if Jenna hadn't been in the barn when Harriet arrived?

Our Own Farm

MY PARENTS FINALLY BROKE DOWN AND BOUGHT A farm a week or two after I had finished eleventh grade. They had wanted to move for a while, and I was very determined that we move to a farm. They were happy to get away from the noise of the city. Our house in Cambridge had been right at a stop sign so at all hours of the night people would stop with their music blaring and wake up the entire household. Our new house was great. It was huge, to me anyways. My parents complained that it was small and that our house in Cambridge had been much bigger in comparison, but they were going by the actual measurements and not by all the wasted space which was most of the house back in the city. Our new property had 50 acres, a few acres of brush in the back, a small creek running through it, and a large rustic bridge that crossed over the creek. Close to the house there was an old race track, a few paddocks, and a very large old style bank barn. The barn hosted eight small stalls all along one aisle. There was also a secret room which I eventually turned into my office. When my parents finalized the move, I became very excited. I would most definitely have to get a new horse to keep Cricket company.

At the time I didn't have very much money, if any money, to put towards a new horse. My opportunity came when my farrier Amanda mentioned that there was a horse who looked just like Cricket who was free to a good home. I didn't need much convincing, not that I wanted another standardbred, but I do love the way Cricket looks. When we headed out to have a look at the horse, we found out his name was Jake, and he did look just like Cricket. Jake was quite a bit taller with white spots on his legs, but he was definitely a look-alike. Amanda pointed out which horse he was and I went out to the field to catch him. Jake, however, was too busy chasing a cat to pay any attention to me. It was like he was sure I was out there for any number of other reasons but it definitely had nothing to do with him. After a few minutes he noticed me still trailing behind him and let me halter him. The first day as I played with him in the round pen he did a nice walk, trot, and canter. His canter was very awkward, but he could do it. We set up a low jump and he sailed over it. I knew then and there that he was coming home. Cricket hadn't really caught on to jumping, but Jake was a natural, even without a graceful canter.

When I "bought" Jake he was seven years old. He had been off the track for only a month and still had a beautiful tucked up belly with long lean muscles on his shoulders and haunches. Living with a large group of mares and geldings, he was at the bottom of the hierarchy and was literally terrified of the draft horse who seemed to be in charge of their herd. He was ridden twice before he came home, once bareback by my daring farrier and once under saddle by the folks who were his owners at the time. We arrived to pick up Jake about two weeks after our family had moved onto the farm. I was with Jill, a lady who was trailering for us and who also boarded at Spooky Ridge Stables where I had kept Cricket. Jill had a small two-horse trailer. The little bumper pull had a divider down the centre to stop the horses from kicking at each other or leaning against one another. We had started out at Spooky Ridge Stables and had already wrapped Cricket's legs and loaded him up. While we were stopped to get Jake we let Cricket come off and play in the round pen. Cricket had already managed to make his wraps slip down, so Jill rewrapped his legs while I wrapped Jake. We loaded Cricket back to the section he had been in before, and we did the butt bar up so that he couldn't scoot out. Then we worked on loading Jake. I guess Cricket didn't like the idea of sharing his transportation, because as soon as Jake was on the ramp Cricket kicked out and even let out a squeal. No one got hurt though, and eventually with the help of many outgoing bystanders (the barn staff were all out there saying goodbye to Jake and clucking and kissing to encourage him to go in) we did have both horses on board. I then went to find the previous owner. She hadn't been around and I wasn't feeling confident about driving off with a horse with no papers, no contract, and no money being exchanged. I found her in an office, but she was busy on the phone and looked at me like I was interrupting the most important phone call of her life. So instead of intruding any further I mentioned to the man who was also in the office that we were leaving with Jake now and just thought I'd let them know. He said that was fine and we departed.

The farm my parents had bought was beautiful, but some things hadn't been kept up. The paddocks and pasture had been left for a long time through a hard divorce. With the property being for sale for quite some time, the grass had grown up past my hip. My dad had attended an auction earlier at the farm where the previous owners had sold off farming equipment, tools, and household objects that they didn't want to move. He had made a few contacts there and among those was an older beef farmer. This man thought it would be a great idea to generously lend us his cows to cut the grass down so that it would be easier for the horses. In hindsight, this probably wasn't a very good idea.

Jake doesn't like cows.

Cricket had never seen cows.

Cows do not respect fences - electric, or of any other sort.

The cows attracted so many flies that the horses were miserable even after they had gotten over the initial shock of a new place (with scary man-eating cows who could break into their section of the fence and chase them when they pleased).

The cows stayed for about two weeks. The cows' owner came by regularly to repair the electric fencing, and I lay on a lawn chair by the road reading magazines to deter the young bulls from escaping towards the road. This at least made it easier to herd them back if they did escape. I got a bit of fresh air and sun, though the neighbours must have thought we were nuts from day one.

It was heaven though. Every night I'd lay in my bed right in front of the window and watch the horses graze. I'd fall asleep with the sound of them quietly walking around the field. Of course, I was just as paranoid as a new mother. I woke up on a regular basis to see if they were still in their field. Every morning when I went outside, Cricket would nicker his adorable 'hello' nicker and then start his more demanding 'where's my food' nicker. It made me smile every day. There is no better way to end your day and then start a new one. My summer went by way too fast. I barely had enough time to train both horses and get settled into our new house. I managed to get a part-time job working for a horse dealer nearby. I mucked stalls once or twice a week and occasionally groomed horses before a sale. Every once in a while, Will, the boss, would bring in a horse he thought I'd like and would try a sales pitch on me. I couldn't really show any interest though, as I wasn't allowed to get another horse.

When school was back in session I started my grade 12 year at a new school. I went from a very large school of 4000 students to a 302-student school, the last two being my brother Brian and myself. Ninety-five percent of the students had been in the same class since they were knee-high to a grasshopper. They'd ridden the same bus their whole lives and they knew everybody and everybody's business. Let me correct that: they knew everybody's and everybody's uncle's cousin's business.

The bus was one thing, as none of us kids had ever ridden a bus. We'd always walked to school. The bus wasn't bad for the most part. The bus driver was very friendly. The girls were gossip queens, the boys were busy talking about the girls, and the little kids made a lot of noise at the front of the bus. That's the way it worked: the older you were, the further back on the bus you were allowed to sit. The ride wasn't very long - just down our road, up another, and back to the school. The high school kids got dropped off first and then the primary grades were taken to the other school.

When I started at the new school I made a promise to myself: I wasn't going to be shy or meek. I was going to walk in on my first day, be confident, and snag the hottest boy in my grade. It was a silly goal, but it made me walk in a little taller, talk a little louder, and even participate more in classes. Within two weeks I was dating one of the hottest boys in grade 12. I was pleased with myself and tried to continue the confident outgoing self I had tried to be from the first day. The boy I was dating was a nice guy who worked on his parents' dairy farm and enjoyed working around the animals. I think he even came to a horse show with a bunch of other guys from school to cheer me on. But then we weren't meant for each other. About two months into the relationship, we broke it off. I was dumped for not wanting to become more seriously involved. After being dumped by one of the most popular people in school, my circle of friends diminished. My confidence went down the drain and I had to press restart yet again.

I had played trumpet all through grades nine to eleven and I stayed with it during my final year of high school. Our teacher was also new to the school so we were able to relate to the new city together. He had specialized in trumpet and would give me extra help or tips. The other trumpet players in our class had been taught by the same teacher and had a lot of flaws with their playing, so it turned out that in comparison to them I was actually great at something, even if it was music, which was considered nerdy to the country clan at the school. I had also excelled in art in Cambridge, but here the teacher was upset with my paintings of horses, sketches of horses, doodles of horses, and models of horses. Basically I could do a horse and receive an average mark, or do anything but a horse and receive a decent mark. She didn't like what I felt my talent was (horses!) and she would lose her cool over anything going differently than what she had envisioned. For instance, a paintbrush put in hair side down into a glass storage jar would cause her to scream at the entire class for more than three minutes. Scrap paper on the floor would result in an intense lecture about materials and costs. If anyone were to ever make a comment or pose a question or concern, she would bite their heads off. Some people are crazy because of things that have happened to them. I would never wish for something to happen to this lady, as I was sure she had been through enough. But I did wish that she'd find another profession. Perhaps factory work or cleaning offices would have suited her creative style better. It's hard enough to keep good subjects in school, and she went along dismissing the creative styles and ideas of the hundreds of students who over the years had to deal with her.

Of course I had been spoiled by my art teachers in Cambridge. All of them had been caring. They had pushed my boundaries, made me think, helped me learn, and given me projects that would involve thought processes and imagination. They'd shown me how or why, explained things, and never, ever dismissed my ideas. These were real teachers, and real teachers are hard to come by and even harder to keep around. Teaching isn't an easy profession; it's a job that wears you down very easily. Sure you get most of the summer off, but can you imagine having to deal with half the kids you went to school with? If your high school experience was anything like mine, you can't and you don't even want to think about it.

When the time came to apply to colleges and universities, I wasn't sure what I wanted to go through for. I knew it was horse-related, but there were not a lot of colleges or universities that offered horse training or coach preparation courses. I researched many of the United States' colleges and found that horses was an additional course you could take after you'd completed a major in something else. There was Olds College in Alberta, but it was mostly Western-based and Alberta seemed too far to go. Kemptville College by process of elimination became my only real choice. It was approximately six hours away, and I could bring my horse. When I was done I'd walk away with a coaching license and a stable management certificate.

When I was accepted to Kemptville I decided to take Jake with me. In the back of my mind I couldn't stand it if something happened to Cricket. Jake was more athletic and would be able to jump, whereas Cricket had decided long ago that jumping wasn't for him. Jake was also better at cantering. Even though he wasn't trained to the same point as Cricket, he seemed to have more potential to go further. Cricket was happy to do a walk and trot, occasionally go on a trail ride, or compete at a show in the fun classes.

Coby

ONCE IT WAS DECIDED THAT CRICKET WOULD BE staying at home, it was also decided that Cricket would need a friend. Will McDougal heard about this and quickly called me with his first prospect. The phone call went like this:

Will: Hey Steph, it's Will McDougal, hey listen, I think I've got a horse for you.

Steph: Oh really, what is it?

Will: Three-year-old stud colt; I think he's a standardbred.

Steph: Hmm, well I don't really want another standardbred.

Will: No, you need to come have a look at him. I'm going to St. Jacobs tomorrow, and I'd rather not take him with me. Come on out and have a look; he might be just the horse for you.

...and that was that.

I convinced my parents much the same way by using guilt that the horse would definitely go to meat if he was a standardbred stud, and what if he was actually a decent horse? My parents bought it. We went out together to look at him. My dad came along to say no to me making an impulse buy, and my mom came along to say no to my dad for letting me make an impulse buy. You'd figure with the two of them backing each other up I wouldn't be coming home with a three-year-old might-a-could-a-been standardbred stud colt.

However...

We met Scoobi who was close to 16 hands at that point. He walked out all proud of himself in a new place and stood tied to the wall while I tried to pick up his feet. He didn't understand, but he wasn't mean and he tried to accommodate my wishes. I brushed him all over which took a while as he pranced a bit. He was covered in woolly winter fur, burs, and mud. I was undecided at that point. I liked his temperament, but he wasn't trained for very much and was quite big to work with. Finally I asked if we could see him move. The deciding moment came when he got all rank on Will leading him. He picked up his feet high and tried to muscle his way through Will. He didn't get away with it and ended up in a puddle. This allowed us to see some real movement. Scoobi then got the stud chain over his nose. He smartened up and walked and trotted beside Will like a gentleman.

This is the point where I turned to my parents and said, "Can I get him?"

They reluctantly agreed.

Scoobi was renamed Coby. His previous owner called me later on in the week and couldn't stop thanking me. She said he had come from out west as a weanling from a PMU farm. PMU stands for Pregnant Mare Urine, which is collected and used to make hormone medication for women. The mares are hooked up to machines for much of the pregnancy where their urine is collected. The foals from the mares are then sold at rock bottom prices across the country to whoever is brave enough to purchase a baby with little to no training. These farms have nearly all gone out of business with synthetic medication taking over in a much more humane way. She told me he had been turned out with sheep for the past two-and-a-half years and that he liked to be pet, but because he kept jumping fences and chasing sheep he had to be sold. She had been very upset with her husband for selling to Will, even though he had assured her he would find the horse a home. I told her that the horse had nearly missed his home as we had purchased him only a day before the auction. I was convinced that Coby wasn't a standardbred, and so I asked her what she thought he was. She said Percheron for sure, but crossed, and she wasn't sure with what. My best guess is a Morgan because he had tiny little ears and for being the size that he was, he was very compact.

Kemptville

COLLEGE CAME UP FAST EVEN THOUGH I WAS PACKED weeks ahead of time. I polished my saddle and bridle and made sure everything I could possibly need was packed in Jake's tack trunks. I had been lucky enough to find a group of students heading down to Kemptville together, so I joined their group and we arranged for a professional horse hauler to come pick us all up at our home farms. The trip started out at my house. Jake was the first one to board a trailer big enough for six horses and as much corresponding tack that you could ever use. Even the truck was roomy and most of my belongings went with me. My dad drove down separately with my clothes and comforters. Our second stop was to pick up Tina and her huge quarter horse. Bred to be a halter horse, he looked very elegant and resembled more of a warmblood than an old fashioned quarter horse. He loaded on fine and we were off to pick up the next horse who was large, mostly draft, and very young. He was a little bit harder to convince to get on the trailer, but in the end he got on. Our last step was to pick up someone else who wasn't going to the school but was having her horse shipped out towards Quebec.

This farm was huge and it was all grass, but not fenced in for the horses. It was really there just to look good. Much like golf courses, this was a waste of good pasture land. This last horse was a chubby little Morgan pony. He was more interested in eating the lush grass we were parked on than in getting on the trailer, but soon enough we were all packed in and on the road again. We had been on the road for nearly 11 hours by the time we started seeing signs on the highway towards Kemptville. When we were just a half hour away from the school, our driver pulled over suddenly onto the gravel shoulder.

Wait, before I go any further I need to describe our lovely drivers. We had a middle aged lady who ran the show; she had organized the trip and she was constantly answering her phone and returning calls. The other was an older man who actually drove trucks for a living; he was just helping out his friend for this short haul, as he referred to it. He was driving during this last leg of our trip when he had slowed down and pulled off the road.

We had been pulled over by a cop. She wasn't impressed with our license plates. We hadn't noticed of course, but the trailer license was an out of province plate (an American plate to be more specific) and the truck was an Ontario plate. The cop kept looking for ways to get us for everything from what we were hauling, to where, and why. The gentleman driver was fined for not having a log book filled in. Since he was a truck driver he was required to drive with a log book when hauling a load that big. Our lady driver was frazzled and tried many ways of talking her way out of this situation. She said that he was just a friend driving for her and that she had driven most of the way, and she said that that they had just gotten the trailer and hadn't had the plates switched between trips. Her attempts at persuasion didn't work, and they got fined even more. Finally, with the horses impatiently stomping in the back, we were on our way again. We got to the school safely and very happy that the trip was over. Jake nearly jumped off the trailer he was so happy to be off of it. And so began our K-Ville adventures.

Kemptville did a lot of things right. Their facility was gorgeous. The main indoor arena, which had been converted from an old hockey arena, was large with kickboards all the way around and enough seating for big events. It had full length mirrors across one of the short sides so that you could see yourself as you were riding. The best feature was that the arena was heated, so all through the winter we could have gotten away with riding in tank tops - not that the instructors would have allowed that.

Each horse had its own 12x12 stall where it could see its neighbours. There were rules all over the place from how to hang up your blanket to when you could have a blanket on your door. The rules were enforced by fees and fines. All these rules kept everything organized and with 80-100 horses it needed to be organized.

Where Kemptville went wrong was the actual instruction, the barn management, and the course structures. If I had known it was going to be a basic pony club review all year, would I have chosen differently and opted not to go? Probably not. Lots of people had told me that it would be a waste of time and I had gone anyway. I couldn't believe that a course specializing in horses could be a waste of time. I enjoyed the college experience, especially the part where I got to stay awake all night drinking, dancing, or just talking and laughing with friends. In the dorms there weren't as many rules and my roommate and I got along great.

The biggest problems came with Jake and the barn management. Jake was put on the morning turnout schedule. This meant he could go out at 8 o'clock and had to be in by noon. Unfortunately Jake became hyper and even aggressive from being locked in a stall too long. We had to cut him completely off of grain in an attempt to keep his energy level under control. With that he lost weight drastically. So then we had to improvise. We started him on beet pulp and worked on keeping his energy level down by using him in every lesson, club, demonstration, or activity we could find. Anything requiring a horse, Jake was the one. He learned quickly to stand for hours while college kids wrapped polos again, and again, and again. He got to be the massage therapy horse and the aroma therapy horse (the scent that put him to sleep was lavender and honey). He was often ridden three times a day, but this still wasn't enough. Jake was so frustrated with his turnout situation that no amount of exercise could keep him focused. In each ride he would bolt and take off across the ring. Sometimes it was because the arena door had opened or someone was walking on the other side of the hockey rink style boards, but often there was no reason to spook. Yet he would launch into the biggest leap sideways and then take off leaping and bucking until he hit something that was strong enough to physically stop him. I managed to stay on every time. I may have been around his neck with my legs up over my head by the end of his run, but I'd still be on. I tried different techniques to get him to stop. The emergency stops he just ran through, and riding and pushing him on would just encourage him. Soon I started a rule: every time he bucked he got a slap on the rump with the crop. So off we'd go bucking and slapping across the ring. At one point he spooked so bad he took off, got a few bucks in, leaped over a pony with a rider, got a couple more bucks in, hit the wall, stopped, reared, and then tried to take off again. This was the last time he got away with it. When he reared I lost my temper and slapped him across both shoulders as hard and as fast as I could, completely sibling style. He got the message. He turned his head as if to ask "What do you want then?" and

I told him trot. I said it aloud and with my legs on and he did; he went into a beautiful floating dressage trot. Now if he even thinks about bucking, I dare him. I put my hands forward and say "Go ahead." He doesn't. On the contrary, he actually puts himself together like the dressage horse he is and goes right to work. You can almost hear him say "I didn't mean it."

Jake and I were constantly getting into trouble at Kemptville. I'd leave him out too long (because he needed to be outside to keep from going completely insane), and then I'd find a hefty fine waiting for me on the stall door. We couldn't even get along with our instructors. My first instructor put us on a circle, said "put your heels down," and left. She walked away and coached the other students for the remainder of the lesson. This happened many times. Finally I went to the head coordinator to try to get transferred to a new coach. After some hassle they did, but this coach was very pregnant and left within two weeks to go on her leave. I was then switched to another coach who was really great and finally got us focused on jumping. She was also the one who wrote a note to the barn management so that Jake could get approved for all day turnout. Thank you!

Through all of this switching of coaches, I was preparing for my Coach 1 exam which would be tested through the Ontario Equestrian Federation. Not. But I was supposed to be preparing. As my horse wasn't jumping the 2'6 requirement, the instructors figured we weren't aiming to go through the exam. They stopped supporting and directing me towards achieving my certificate. At that point I should have started yelling and stomping my feet, you know the squeaky wheel gets the grease idea, but I didn't. We were put out of the picture and the instructors forgot about us. Eventually I forgot about it as well, especially when my only other option would have been to jump a green broke horse that the school offered for use in lessons. So then the last and final option was to become just an instructor. This is basically a glorified trail guide. I decided against this at the end of the year simply because I had become frustrated with the whole entire program. Out of my class of approximately 60 students, only three became certified coaches. In this regard the college experience was a waste.

Luckily that's not all it was. I made some great friends and pushed myself emotionally through a rough patch. I had fallen in love with a boy from home who really didn't want anything to do with me unless I acted like I wanted nothing to do with him. It was just a game to him, but I spent many nights crying myself to sleep because I just couldn't get him out of my mind. Michaela my roommate was amazing to me; she stayed up late at night and talked me through a lot of my grief. I tried to do the same for her on her rough days, but she definitely helped me more.

During the school year I was asked out by Peter, a good friend of mine. I declined by making all sorts of excuses - he wasn't my type, or no, I just didn't feel the same. He didn't take the rejection well, but by the end of the year he was happily dating another friend of ours. The three of us and about five others spent many nights together singing along to country songs, going out dancing, and spinning around in their vehicles in the snow. We were constantly getting sound warnings and being told to keep the party inside the room. After ten it was supposed to be quiet in the dorms, but that rarely happened regardless of where on the campus you were. While I was at college I kept my mind goal-oriented even with all the fun I was having. Was I going to be able to get a stable going at my parents' place? How was I going to compete against the other stables in the area? What were my next steps? I decided to start horse hunting. My school loan had an extra bit of money on it so for once I wasn't hunting with empty pockets. I searched for the perfect beginner horse. Cricket is an excellent beginner horse. He carefully guesses what the student wants, he doesn't spook unless it's something really scary, and he doesn't go faster than they're ready for, even if they think they're ready. But I didn't want Cricket to be stuck with every beginner who came out. As my first horse he is very special to me. Beginners ruin horses with their heavy hands, their sack of potatoes balance, and their nagging legs. So my goal was to find a horse that could shoulder at least some of Cricket's burden so that he'd get a break and stay happy working.

Polly-Anne came up in a search on Equestrian Connection, an online horse classifieds site. She was a pretty chestnut mare who was 15.2 hands high and a thoroughbred. She had raced as a two-year-old, had a couple of babies, and then competed in hunter on the A circuit for a couple of years before the current owner had purchased her to use as a broodmare. She was $3000 and 19 years old. I didn't have a vehicle, so after a couple of emails I started asking around if anyone would drive me up to Newmarket to have a look at her. Newmarket would take nearly four hours to get to. Peter finally agreed and we left after school was over.

One hundred and eighty-nine km an hour on the 401 in rush hour. That is how I can sum up that trip. We made it in two hours.

Peter is a great driver, I'll give him that, but it was definitely scary. We were incredibly lucky not be pulled over. When we arrived, the stable was just a little farm on a residential street - probably one of the last of its kind in the Toronto area. It was already dark and snow had started falling. By the light of one flood light on a shed we were able to see the horse out with her buddies in frozen over muddy paddocks. She was tall and thin with a beautiful white blaze and odd white markings on her leg. Unlike most stockings, hers didn't go all the way to the ground; instead, it was a painted splash on her leg. I wanted to ride her, but they didn't have a saddle. I sat on her bareback instead and had the owner lead me around a bit. I played with my legs and Polly-Anne moved off of the pressure with the slightest touch. I don't think I even trotted her because the footing was too icy. Polly-Anne was spooked by being out in the dark away from her friends, but she dealt with me being on her back and playing with her mane. For some reason this was enough to convince me she was the right horse. I do have good luck with horses, so I followed my gut and purchased her that day. I offered $2000 and the owner accepted, and then I paid an extra $500 to keep her at the location until school term was up. Once all the arrangements were made and we were on our way, it was past 11 p.m.

Peter didn't speed on the way home because the roads were becoming too icy. We stopped at a gas station and Peter bought a scratch card and an iced tea. We also ordered some food. As we sat and ate, Peter told me how he'd won a lottery when he was younger. He had used the money to pay his father's farm off and to purchase a new truck. The new truck wasn't going to be touched until he put an undercoating on it three times. He even got it delivered to his house so that there wouldn't be any miles on it at all. On our way again, Peter was becoming more and more tired. By the time we were within a half hour of Kemptville, he couldn't stay awake anymore so we switched and I drove. This was my first time ever driving a truck and we were on the highway. I was so terrified, I even shook. I know I probably asked a million questions before we were on the road again. I was trying to figure out where the lights were and how to adjust my seat so I could reach the pedals. Once I got going it wasn't too bad and I quickly got used to driving a truck. The roads weren't busy at all and the odd car we did come across passed us without any trouble. I may have been going a tad slower than the speed limit. After parking at the school I was so full of adrenaline I didn't get to sleep until well past four.

The next day I told my parents about the new purchase. They weren't thrilled, as I was already in debt from school, but I convinced them that it was a good idea to have another beginner horse for the lesson program. This would be the program that I would put all my efforts into when I returned home after the semester. Now or never. Jump in with both feet. Go big or go home. These are the types of inspirational sayings that twirled through my head every day.

Coming Home

WELL, I MADE IT THROUGH COLLEGE ALIVE. I DID THE trip home with Jake, picked up our new Polly-Anne, and made it home before dark. We put Polly-Anne and Jake outside in the riding ring to play and after a long ride home together they were already friends. They had a good time stretching their legs before they went in for the night. I don't usually put horses inside; I hate it really. But since Polly-Anne was new and didn't know the property, I put her in for the night just this once.

There are so many reasons not to put a horse inside that I could write an entire book on the conflicts of horse management. I won't. But since I have your attention, I will mention a few key details that make me lean towards keeping my horses outside. First and most importantly is air circulation. The number one reason why meat rabbits, meat goats, beef cattle, and chickens die or become ill is lack of proper ventilation. One thing that did stick with me from college is if you have an in-vent that's a start, but it won't do much good until you have an out-vent so that the air actually has a path to travel. Just like water. Unless you have somewhere for it to go, it's going to just keep coming in. So the same concept applies to the horses. Basically if you walk into a barn and you're used to the usual barn smells but you can smell the urine, then there is not enough ventilation! Basic easy fix...open a window. Common sense that isn't so common. Next key point is circulation. Not air circulation, I've already said enough about that, but the horse's actual circulation. When you are forced to sit or stand for a long period of time say at work or at school, you get tired and sore. Your muscles start to fall asleep, you get cranky, and in the end you stare out the window aimlessly instead of doing anything productive. I worked an office job at one point in my life. I worked an eight-hour day and had a twenty-minute lunch and two five-minute breaks throughout the day. My muscles hated me. I became so stiff I almost limped. That's a bit of an exaggeration compared to most people who are comfortable sitting in an office, but I wasn't used to it. Horses are the same way: indoors isn't normal for them (nor me!), and they aren't used to standing or laying all day. Out in the wild they stand, graze, run, saunter, lay down, roll, chase, play, snort, rear, buck, kick etc. etc. etc. etc. What is normal about being locked up?

So I made it home, I had a new horse, and I had decided to get my new lesson stable going with the help of a part-time job at Subway. Any true business person will tell you that it takes at least three years to develop a business that will support itself. So in the meantime I worked Subway to pay for my hay, grain, farrier, and vet. I lived on a strict budget and mooched off of my parents as much as possible. My parents were great as always, and so my food and rent were covered. I got in trouble and yelled at from time to time for not helping enough around the house, and was very often threatened that if I didn't do the chore in question I'd be paying rent. If I didn't like what we were having for supper, then I could buy my own food. I heard that one a lot. I'm a bit of a picky eater.

My first students came as a result of Kijiji ads or posters I had put up in shops in town. I'd grow my business to half a dozen students but by winter be down to none as it was too cold or too icy to ride outdoors. I kept my prices below other stables in the area to attract a few clients. But even with just the four horses, the business never made enough to support itself. I knew that even while I was doing it, but I wasn't ready to give up.

In fall of 2008 my mother and I went on an outing. We have days that I fondly call Mommy-Stephi days. They are always a special time, even if we don't do anything special. Usually we do a lot of driving, a lot of talking, and my mom treats me to ice cream, coffee, and maybe even a meal or two. I always feel spoiled. I know she did the same outings with her mom and her grandmother, so it feels like a tradition. We rarely even feel guilty about this luxury because it is such a tradition.

This particular time I convinced my mom to go to the live-stock exchange in St. Jacobs. We walked around on the top floor looking down at all the sorry looking standardbreds, the overworked draft horses, and the assortment of backyard bred horses and ponies. My eyes came across the back of a Palomino Haflinger. I wrote the horse's number down on the back of my bidding number and just told my mom that this was the horse that had attracted my eye the most. I liked the way the back was shaped, nothing more. I couldn't see very much and I wasn't really interested in going down as nothing had piqued my inter-est. I always write down the numbers of the horses I like, but I never end up getting anything. I wrote down two more numbers: one was a standardbred who was built small like Cricket and the other was a beautiful gray who looked like an Andalusian stallion the way he held himself. But he was three-legged lame and so I knew he wouldn't bring much and would end up in the kill pen. It killed me watching him walk down the aisle; he was basically my dream horse, and he had a sweet eye. I couldn't believe someone could do that to such a beautiful horse. We left, sat down in the auction bleachers, and watched almost all of the horses go through before the Haflingers came in. Two of them were announced as full sisters, both three years old. (That would mean twins, so the audience chuckled lightly at that description.) The one mare looked right at me and I just had a feeling she was the right horse. I told my mom right then that I wanted that horse. I asked if I could bid on her. The end call was always up to my parents, as it was their farm and their rules. Mom agreed too easily. I should tell you that she had been going through a tough time with her health. She had been given a cancer scare and the doctors hadn't yet confirmed if it was a tumor or not. A few years earlier my mom had lost her own mom to ovarian cancer. The timing was very scary for her. So she basically went into a midlife crisis at that exact moment and said, "Sure, why not, buy the horse."

I bid, and the bid kept going up. It finally stopped at over five hundred, which I couldn't afford, so I had to let it go. The auctioneer had said it was first choice, so first bidder could have his choice of mare. A young Amish man had outbid me. He thought quickly and then choose the bigger of the two because she'd likely be a year older. I was relieved; my mare was still for sale! The bidding began again and finally ended at $425 with me calling out my bidder's number. I was thrilled. Will, who was there as well, offered to trailer her home. The previous owner came up to my mother as I was watching her being ushered into another holding area. He told her they'd taught her to lead this morning by tying her to the old tractor. Had to do it to get her on the trailer. He then warned me that the horse was wild, barely handled.

"I don't want you getting hurt," he repeated a few times.

He asked if we were interested in any more as he was getting too old to be breeding horses, and my mom panicked and said "no" too fast. Then he left before I could get any information on bloodlines or registration possibilities. I think she was shocked at the tractor story. I know I was! Some horses survive so much.

We took our time getting home. I called Dad and gave him a fair warning that we'd been up to something. We stopped at the tack shop and splurged on a lot of pink grooming equipment and then a yarn shop as well for my mom since she loves to knit. When we arrived home the horse was already in a stall and looked more adorable than I had imagined. She was small, only about 12.3 hands - a Palomino with a large white blaze. What made her unique was that inside the white blaze were two half moon shapes in the palomino colouring. She was shy but I went inside the stall and pet her. She was okay with that so I started grooming her. I groomed her entire body and even picked up her hooves. She kept her eyes on me the whole time, but already there was a trust building between us. For having barely been handled I have never seen a horse respond that quietly. Thinking back she must have been in shock, but that little mare let me do just about anything to her. I found many little lumps all over her skin. I assumed they were hives from the stressful day, but over the next week they didn't go away. I consulted a vet and they eventually came out and confirmed that it was a bad case of rain rot. It was so bad in fact that we had to put her on antibiotics for two weeks and treat her once a day with an iodine concoction for the next few months. She hated me for that. I was constantly picking at the scabs and currying the skin as hard as I could. I hated that I had to do it. To this day she despises baths, but she has nice clear skin. So hey - you win some, you lose some. We named the pony Portia. We had thought of a lot of names and

I had narrowed it down to about ten which included the likes of Daisy and Pebbles. Then I remembered a friend of Peter's named Porteah who was an amazing artist and had even drawn up a tattoo sketch for me. So I sent her a Facebook message asking if I could essentially steal her name. She was happy to share but insisted I spell it Portia because it was much cooler, and I am happy she did. Portia suits the pony perfectly, although we still refer to her as "the pony" on a regular basis. A year later we had a contest at our stable to come up with a show name for her. Portia Wanna Ride became the winner, and Tia, as we now call her for short, has shown under this name in everything from Pony Hunters, to Western Pleasure, to speed events (including Craig Cameron's Extreme Cowboy Race). Tia is the type of horse who gets bored easily, so I am constantly trying to find new things to teach her.

Portia learned quickly to lunge, and was completely fine with a saddle and bridle. All along I kept thinking that if this horse is so good she's going to do something insane when I go to ride her. I think someone had said something along those lines to me when I was a lot younger and the warning had stayed with me regardless of whether it carried any merit. Always watch the quiet ones; you don't know what they're thinking. Could this apply to me too? I'm a quiet one, does that mean I could be a danger? I doubt many are worried about that with me.

I follow a lot of different horse trainers online. One man I am very fond of is short and athletic with dark hair, blue eyes, and an Australian accent. He posts on YouTube quite often with his newest projects. One video showed a horse who would rear straight up in the air and wouldn't quit. He taught it not to, simply by letting it rear all it wanted while just staying with him - out of the way but still on his back. Eventually the horse got tired of rearing and just stopped. At this point he made the horse halt and didn't allow it to walk away until he decided. For whatever reason, this worked, and the horse didn't even attempt to rear at all for the next few days. He just trotted out past the barns without even looking like he wanted to rear. Now this was a completely different attitude to horse training. This man also invented a technique where he lays the horse down very quickly and quietly just by putting them into a position where laying down is the easiest thing to do. The horse becomes very quiet and much less resistant. He uses this technique a lot with different rank horses and can generally get them to be calm and responsive within minutes. I chose to try this technique for two reasons. The first was to learn it as it seems to have magical powers over the most furious of horses, and the second was to make sure the little pony of mine didn't have any tricks up her sleeve.

It took me a lot longer to figure out how to accomplish what I had seen in the videos, but being as it was my first attempt I'm sure I wasn't doing it perfectly. I did get Portia down, and I did it a couple more times before I decided to ride her. All the time she was quiet, responsive, and didn't mind laying down. Even further, she didn't mind me being on top of her. When I encouraged her to stand up, she did so without a fuss and simply glanced around at me to see what I was doing. Maybe this just goes to prove what a tolerant and patient horse I have, but perhaps this had something to do with the new training tools I had learned. I definitely decided to keep this idea in my toolbox. I could see this being the step the original horse trainers used to do before the Western world of trainers gave laying a horse down a bad rep by making them fall down from essentially tripping them. There are good ways to do all horse training. Whenever you are working on a horse and you come to an issue, stop and ask yourself, "Why am I asking this way?" Are you skipping steps? Can you make the step you're asking into a smaller step? What exactly do you want your horse to do, and why is this method the best for this particular horse?

My Shadow

IN THE SPRING I STARTED INTO MY FIRST REAL MEAN-
ingful relationship with a human...rather than a horse. His
name was Calabe and he was three years older than me. The
first time I met him I was working at The Beer Store in Ayr.
We had a strict policy that we were to ID anyone who we suspected was under the age of 30. The drinking age is 19; however,
if you guessed at a person's age and you were off by 10 years,
at least this way you could still catch any who were underage.
This policy was slightly overkill but a necessary part of the job.
Calabe came in and when I asked for his ID, he snottily said,
"I'm old enough to be your father." That cocky attitude turned
out to be the only reason I was attracted to him. He wasn't bad
looking, but he wasn't attractive to me. He had nice eyes and a
nice smile but he was overweight and his hair was already reced-
ing. But personality-wise we clicked. I could talk all I wanted,
and he would listen and even pay attention to what I was saying
like it mattered. I could talk about anything at all (mainly
horses), and he would nod, smile, and agree with everything I
said. Together we truly had something in common: we loved to

attend animal auctions. Occasionally he would take some of his father's birds to sell, mainly ducks or chickens. At every auction we brought home more than we took. I eventually had my own rabbit-breeding business started in the barn with miniature Rex (very soft short-haired), Lionhead (long hair around their heads like a lion's mane), and Dutch (short-haired black with a white stripe around the belly). Calabe started his own business too - he raised Flemish Giants. By the name you can guess that they are giant rabbits. His main buck was at least 40 pounds and when I held him I had to carry him like a medium-sized dog. His ears alone were at least the length of my fingertips to my elbow.

In May we attended an event held in Mount Forest called the Fur and Feather. This is a gathering of every animal you can think of (pet-sized) around the town's baseball fields on a running track. Everyone brings their critters, animal products, or accessories and buys, sells, and trades. It doesn't start until 8 a.m. but to get a spot on the track you need to be there by 6. We left Calabe's parents house at 5:30 a.m. loaded up with chickens, ducks, and rabbits of every size and colour. Calabe brought cue cards and highlighters to write down prices and information for each animal. Calabe's dad drove and we crammed ourselves in the truck amongst all the animals and cages. When we arrived it was still dark and the track was already full of vendors. We parked sideways in a small spot between two larger vehicles who had to move their inventory just to fit us in. We spent the morning taking turns at our "booth" and wandering the track looking at other animals. I bought a couple of rabbits who were better quality than what I was selling, and I was happy with my purchases. Then Calabe and I took over at the truck and Calabe's dad went off to shop. When he came back he asked if we had seen the Rottweiler puppy. We hadn't, so we went off again and came across a cute little black puppy with a big head and little tan paws. The owner wasn't there but her parents were and said she wanted $100. He was the last of the litter. I thought the puppy was cute but I wasn't sold on him - that is until I picked him up and he licked my face.

His name was B-boy, named by the owner's kids after the basketball dog that starred in some movie about a dog who plays basketball. He was just five weeks old. I paid exactly $85 for him, most of which I borrowed from Calabe with strong convincing. Calabe tried to talk me out of it; he knew my parents had said absolutely no dogs. But I was the happiest girl in the world! We walked about halfway around the track before a real name came to me: Rascal. I said it out loud and it was right. Rascal has been my shadow ever since. It's funny because although no animal could ever replace Cricket, Rascal seems to be just as special but in a different part of my heart. It's like my heart grew to accommodate loving a dog just as much as my horse.

It took longer for my dad's heart to accept the dog though. Rascal lived in the barn and wasn't allowed inside the house under any circumstances. My dad didn't speak to me for a week. I eventually approached him in his office while he was working because I couldn't stand the tension any longer. He was disappointed. He was angry. And his closing statement was "and you just don't need a dog." Which was true in one sense, as a few months later I ended up thousands of miles away from my dog. But in the way that counts I do need a dog. I did need a dog. He kept me active and happy. He would always look for me and come running as soon as he saw me. We would play fetch all day long, go for runs or walks together, bike, or roller blade. When my dad was working in his home office I would sneak Rascal into my bedroom and we would sleep together. For a very long time he didn't find out, as by morning we would be up and out the door. Rascal knew we were doing something naughty; I could tell because he wouldn't whine or bark but would just crawl into bed beside me. He was smart right from the start. His previous owner had told me that Rascal's father was very smart. He would do everything from picking up the telephone to opening the fridge and grabbing a beer. I had hoped my dog would be that smart, but I got even better than that. Rascal doesn't open the fridge and help himself to whatever is inside; instead, he has manners. He waits patiently for each and every person in the house to be fed before he even nibbles, including the cats. He knows which horse is which even though they are almost all the exact same colour. He plays cop dog each day. When a horse is misbehaving all I have to do is shout their name and Rascal runs up and barks at them to knock it off. He has done everything around the barn from leading the horses with their lead ropes to riding them with a leader. He is constantly in the way, but I wouldn't have it any other way.

Slowly, over time Rascal moved his way into the house, and with my mom on his side he eventually made himself an indoor dog all together. To this day he continues to be my shadow.

Part 2

Internship

A FEW MONTHS AFTER RASCAL CAME INTO MY LIFE I received an email asking if I was still interested in an internship I had applied to. The internship was in Nebraska to train for three months with Darius Rodriguez. Living accommodations were provided and I would be fed while on the road with Darius and his crew. After three months there would be a possibility of being hired on and paid to stay longer. I had sent my resume to them a few months earlier but I had all but forgotten about the program. I was thrilled when I passed the phone interview and after making arrangements for my animals (begging my parents with all my heart to look after them for three months) I was able to go. It's not every day you get an offer to work with one of the top trick trainers in the world. Reflecting back on this time now I can't even put into words how much I learned in these months that felt like years, yet seemed to pass by in only days.

Calabe drove me down and we arrived in Nebraska at about 10 at night. We found that everyone was busy running a roping competition. After wandering around the huge facility for awhile we finally located Darius and his sister Mary.

The facility had a tack shop on it, a large farmhouse, and three barns all of which are bigger than any I had worked in before. The main barn had a warm up arena on one end and then a long shoot down the middle to a huge competition ring with seating on both sides. There was an overhead office, a full sound system, and a kitchen.

Closer to 11 p.m. we followed Ariel the barn manager through town to a small house that I would be sharing with her. The house was about ten minutes away from the barn and there was absolutely nothing special about it. It consisted of a living room, a narrow standing-room-only kitchen, and three bedrooms just big enough for beds. There was one closet (where we kept a vacuum) and one bathroom. All on one floor. I was happy to find out that Ariel had a dog, a beautiful friendly boxer who didn't mind me moving in. Calabe had to sleep in a separate room (Ariel's rules). He wasn't able to sleep so he left very early in the morning.

My first day started with a lot of stalls. We began with the regular horse stalls belonging to approximately 40 horses. We basically cleaned the stalls with the horses inside them. They were all fairly well-behaved and we would move them around with the fork pointing at their hip and telling them "whoa" when we had them where we needed them. Then we'd move them again to do the other side of the stall. Even the young horses were accustomed to this routine. In his barn Darius had horses of every shape and colour. I wasn't allowed to muck out any stalls containing Darius's show horses. I was actually strictly forbidden to touch any of his horses. His famous trick horses of course were Topaz and Taz, two American Paint horses. Bolt was a mustang that he had picked out himself from a helicopter and trained from wild. Chrome Desire was his heart horse. Okay, he may not have called him that, but you could tell that Chrome Desire was Darius's number one. Parker Joe was an American Paint. In the same aisle he had Jupiter, who was Mary's old trick mare, and a big black Fresian stallion who belonged to Darius's wife (who was also a Mary...). The horses in this aisle were treated with the utmost of care; they had double-wide stalls and deep bedding. In the next aisle were the horses I was allowed to touch. We had Atlas and Alastor, the identical Morgan brothers. There was only one way to tell them apart in that Atlas had slightly smaller more narrow ears. Next was the Paint team, Phoenix and Paladin, and the Haflinger team (pure pony trouble) comprised of Plutus and Hercules. There was a beautiful American Cream Draft horse named Violet. Ariel's two horses were also in this aisle; one was a mustang named Trigger and the other was a thoroughbred. The other stalls consisted of four Rocky Mountain Horses. One was a weanling filly, the next was one or two years old, and the others were three and four year-olds. Two had striking flaxen manes and tails with dark chestnut coats. Chief was another stallion. He was jet black, a pure two-year-old Trekhaner.

When the stalls were done Ariel and I spent the rest of the morning cleaning up the other stalls that had been used for the competition the night before. We then cleaned the bleachers, emptied out the garbage bins, and tidied up the bathrooms and tack rooms. Then we did stalls again for our main forty horses. They were done morning and night without fail. Within the first few days I learned how to harness up the chariot teams. There were two teams: the Paints and the Haflingers. The Morgans used to be a team but were no longer being used. I was required to know the parts of the harness and chariot and be able to harness very quickly and effectively. Once the horses were tied we picked out all their feet from one side rather than moving between the team. For example, Phoenix was the left side horse so when pulling he would be on the left for the driver. When getting them ready we would pick out Phoenix's feet while standing on his left and just reaching across for the right feet rather than walking in between the two horses. I got to ride along inside the chariot while Mary (Darius's sister) was driving. She smelled really good. I know this is a weird thing to be reading but this is a memory of mine and she wore a very unique perfume that you don't easily forget. In a chariot built for one person you tend to stand quite close to the driver as you have no choice. Mary let me try my hand at driving after about fifteen minutes of warming up the team. I took the reins and learned the basics. It isn't much different than riding, as you still want to be gentle on the reins by using them gradually and only as needed but never more. I attempted to learn my vocal commands which included gee and haw (left and right), whoa (well okay I knew that one already), and trot and hup (hup is what they used to get the horse to canter). I often got my gee and haw mixed. I occasionally forgot to turn in time, but I never actually ran the team into anything. I enjoyed driving the teams immensely.

Two days after arriving we were loading up the trailers to leave. Both Darius and Mary had matching trailers with their names and logos covering them from front to back. Darius's was a bigger version but they were equally impressive and fit up to six horses comfortably. We weren't just bringing horses though - we had a full sales booth with t-shirts, training equipment, and even Breyer models of Topaz and Taz. Darius's trailer had to carry the hay on the top of it for the two-week long trip. It also had living quarters and space for all of his performing gear. Among his performance gear there was a huge pedestal that was impossible to pack if you didn't pack it first. I learned all of this the first few days. Of course we couldn't forget his costumes and all of the horses' tack and stable supplies and props (i.e. jumps that light on fire). In Mary's trailer we had to fit in the chariots (almost as hard to pack as the pedestal) as well as extra booth equipment.

Darius left with his wife and Justin (Mary's husband) a day ahead of Mary, Ariel, and myself.

We left at four the next morning. Mary drove the entire way. For the first few hours she cranked the air conditioning to keep herself awake. This was winter. I had been pre-warned by Ariel and had my blankets up front with me. Mary let me talk the whole drive and I hope I was a good passenger. Ariel slept most of the way in the back seat. We were heading down to Ocala Florida for the big horse expo.

Before we got to the expo grounds we stopped for lunch and I met Darius's and Mary's mother. I liked her instantly. She was very pretty just like Mary, and seemed to care about everyone at the table regardless of the fact that I had only been with the team for only a few short days. After lunch we hurried to the expo so that the horses didn't need to wait on the trailer any longer. When we arrived I tried to count the number of horse barns I could see, but I lost count in the process. The expo was huge. There were numerous rings full of brightly coloured jumps. Some rings were used just to store the massive amount of jumps. There were round pens every few barns and outdoor wash stalls at every barn. There were a few small fields for turnout between each barn along with offices, administration buildings, and about a hundred outhouses. After we had unloaded the horses and tack we went to the booth to help them set up. There is a rule when you are setting up a booth at any expo - bring more zip ties. We could never pack enough. I helped set up the displays and then Ariel and I went back to look after the horses. After evening chores were taken care of we were taken to our hotel. We were all staying at different hotels due to a booking schedule that Darius's mother had put together. Basically we got to live like gypsies and we moved hotels three times during our two-week stay. The first hotel was lovely; it was all horse themed. You can guess that Ariel and I were in our element. They had paintings of Lustianos on the wall and a retired carriage horse lived on the property. When you were swimming in the pool you could see him in his own paddock. It was heavenly. If I am ever lucky enough to go back to Florida, I will hunt out this hotel and stay in it as long as possible. The continental breakfast was weak but we watched the news and drank our coffee and ate our stale muffins whenever we could. One evening there was a bit of a panic. The Rodriguez's mom had basically put the expo together herself and had advertised that there were supposedly many more people attending than what was actually expected. She had worked hard to put it together but it was her first try at something this big. The night before the expo started we stayed until nearly midnight putting together welcome packages for companies who would be exhibiting their products there. These packages included information about where their booths were located, the daily schedules, and lots of sponsor information - pretty important stuff. That evening after we had been driven back to the hotel Ariel and I were starving, so we went for a walk, found a Dairy Queen, and got two giant ice creams. It was funny in the morning as I guess Mary and Justin had heard us leave and knew exactly what we had been up to! Working with the Rodriguez family you never had a lot of free time, but when we did Ariel and I would go for walks and explore wherever we were. These breaks weren't really a highlight but more like a breath of fresh air, as Darius is very intense and when you were around him you wanted to make him proud by doing your best, working hard, and working fast. If Darius said run, you ran! Once at a clinic his mic quit on him and I had to run to the office to get a new battery pack. I ran, but no matter how fast I ran I knew he would comment to the audience about me being too slow. And he did. Darius wasn't a kind soul. Darius was a get-it-done-now type of soul.

Darius may not have been kind, but he was good at what he did. There are not very many people who can convince two horses to gallop side by side so that he could stand on their backs... with no equipment. Let me say that again: there was nothing on the horses. He sometimes left a rope around the neck of the quicker horse so that he could reach down and make a correction if he got too fast, but not always. Sometimes he just got on and did it.

One of my favourite days with some of the best memories ever was the last day, the big final performance where all the acts came together and all the performers did their best. The morning practice was uneventful other than me attempting to lead two teams of chariot horses back across the fair grounds to their stalls while being half-dragged the entire time. With two horses in each hand, I got about 60 feet away from the chariot before I yelled to Ariel that I needed help. The Haflinger-Quarter horse crosses were not known to follow rules. Within a few feet they were prancing, and by 60 feet they were turning around towards the other team I was attempting to lead. Luckily I was new and still had Ariel backing me. Leading four horses on your own through a fairground full of noise, tents, excitement, and slamming outhouse doors is not exactly a walk in the park. These horses were experienced, and they sure knew I wasn't. Well, not at that particular task! I found out that the quicker you walked the easier it was to keep the horses' attention. They would assume you were leader and then quickly follow you instead of looking around at things to spook at.

Before the show I spotted Jim, a friend of the Rodriguez's who was driving the Haflinger chariot team in the gladiator race. He was flirting with a very pretty lady who was very obviously not a horse lady. Later that evening he put on the wildest performance of the night. The chariot act is great: it's set to suspenseful dramatic music and has an intense amount of energy. The audience gets to cheer for either Zelda (Mary) or Link (Jim). The race is staged so that it is as safe as possible in a tight arena. First one chariot passes, and then another takes the lead. The announcer does a great job at building the suspense and even to this day this act gives me goose bumps; yes, this is ridiculous, but it's really so exciting. At the end of the race the winner is always Zelda, no doubt about it, but then Link loses control and goes in a zigzag down the middle of the arena. From there his chariot flips and he is catapulted out of it, nearly hitting the horses in front who luckily (and skillfully) become unattached to the wreckage behind them. During this particular performance, Jim, trying to impress his lady friend, drove the Haflingers so fast down the middle that when the chariot flipped he was sent flying 20 feet behind the horses. It was incredible! I was supposed to be "behind the scenes" catching the loose horses who were usually great and loved to come right to me (thank god for carrots)... and I was stunned! Later I overheard a conversation between Mary and Jim.

She was upset and yelled, "Were you trying to get yourself killed?"

Wow, I had thought that's the way the act was supposed to go; alas, yes, but not with that much flying.

A little later on that same night was Darius's act. This was his main act which he had made famous with Chrome Desire. Darius did everything from getting bucked off, chased, falling off, sitting on the horse upside down while playing a song on his hooves, and using the horse's hooves as a helmet rack. Darius was very upset going into the act, as there was supposed to be a shuttle launch literally at the same time. He didn't want his act interrupted; however, there wasn't any point delaying the act as realistically the shuttle launch could end up being delayed. Everyone was flustered; yet they weren't even sure if the shuttle launch was close enough to see it clearly. Darius announced before he started his act that he had arranged for something very special that night, just for his audience. Halfway through the act, Darius paused and lay across his horse's back looking up at the sky. So did the audience. The shuttle was definitely close enough to see; we could even hear it! This was the highlight of the night and Darius, a true performer, made it very special.

There were a lot of bumps on that trip. Darius and his wife had a bad fight that caused all of us to stay awake into the middle of the night. After arriving at the hotel we had to drive right back to the expo to make sure they were okay. Darius's sister Mary was always there to help him out and Darius's wife, although very nice, wasn't the right fit for Darius. Down the road (after I had gone back to Canada) they did eventually split and go their separate ways. I am lucky to be one of the few who are still friends with both. Both are very independent and strong characters.

I learned a lot in Nebraska. I was too busy to be homesick, but I missed my companions Cricket and Rascal the most. I spoke as often as I could with my parents but mostly we just emailed back and forth. Working for Darius was always challenging with early mornings and long days. If we weren't on the road with him, then we were running shows or events at his facility. They hosted barrel racing shows every other weekend and roping events at least once a month. These events always drew a huge crowd. I remember wondering why we don't treat horse sports the same in Canada. It didn't seem right that a person could spend 100 dollars on a stall, a trailer spot, and three barrel runs and then walk away at the end of the weekend a couple hundred dollars ahead. Not to say everyone made money, but a lot of people covered their costs to play and the good riders walked away with money. Horse trainers would take up to six horses, ride them all throughout the day, and cash in between the training fees they'd charge and the money they'd win. Plus there was a jackpot: if you ran a clear round you were entered into it. I worked all sorts of positions when we hosted these events. Often I helped Ariel in the kitchen serving the best burgers on the planet and our own specialty coffee (loads of hot chocolate and whipped cream with a lot of coffee in the middle). The ropers loved our coffee and we made tips on those nights. Barrel racers didn't spend as much on food and drinks, but the ropers were there for a good time. Once Ariel had to go out and buy more food after midnight to keep the riders satisfied. One rider could order three burgers in just one night. The ropers were big, friendly, and rich. We loved working those nights, even though they were long and the mornings came early. The barrel racers weren't as gracious, as they didn't follow rules and would constantly be smoking in the barn or putting more than one horse in a stall they'd paid for to try and save costs.

One morning we came in at 7 o'clock like usual and heard the best whistling in the world. After a few minutes of listening while we fed grain we decided to hunt down whoever the whistler was and we found the vet. He was walking amongst his horses that he would actually be competing with that weekend and just whistling away. I hadn't ever heard even a song bird sound as nice, and that's a lovely memory. He was a very nice vet. I think every once in a while you come across amazing characters in the horse world, just like Cowboy Randy. The vet was definitely one of them. His smile was contagious. Everyone looked out for where he was and paid attention to his racing times. He was like a celebrity.

When the events were over, Ariel and I were really put to the test.

Darius would say "Clean out these stalls by noon and have horses tacked ready for training by one."

After an event with over 200 competitors, we often had over 200 stalls to clean. Even with a skid steer this was a hard task. At the end of the day we would sweep the aisles - four of them, each with twenty stalls (this is just the main barn to give you an idea of the size of the operation I am talking about). Darius had a specific way of sweeping: when we were done any dust left over should be in perfect little straight lines and the job shouldn't take very long at all. How fast does it take you to walk down the row five times? That's how fast it should take to sweep up! It took me a while to get the hang of this. Once after a long day Darius came up and yelled at me for taking 20 minutes to sweep an aisle. Ya, it wasn't that I wasn't trying; I was just damn tired. But I tried and worked harder.

Darius was the type to break you down with work and with words. He would then build you back up. The first few weeks were hard for me, because although I had already trained my own horses, for the first month he didn't even let me touch his horses. Eventually I gained his trust, I believe, because he did let me work with them. One of my first interactions with Taz (one of his highly trained paint horses who did liberty and bridle-less work) was very frustrating. I was told to go clean his stall. The horse was bored out of his mind and happy to see someone new. Taz started playing with me; he started showing me all his tricks. I asked him to move back so that I could clean around him and he'd bow to one knee, or rear, or smile, or salute, or nod or shake. It was like he was going through his repertoire. I spoke with Ariel about this, as I thought it was amazing. But I knew that if Darius saw what Taz was doing he would have thought I was tuning out his very subtle cues. I made Ariel watch me cleaning the stall the next time to make sure I wasn't accidentally cuing him. I wasn't. The horse was just very playful and was showing me what he knew to get my attention. Taz had a bit of a pony attitude. He would be so lazy for Darius in his training sessions but in front of a crowd he would show off and capture everyone's attention. I started to understand why Darius didn't practice often. The horse didn't need the training; he knew his job. It also made me very aware of why Darius didn't allow me to work with his show horses early on. In the future I would often feel the same way Darius did with my own herd. Though I would have wonderful people working with me, they could not understand the training a horse has had and would unknowingly make the cues mean less and less. It's easy to do by asking slightly incorrectly or by not expecting the result with the same quality of movement or enthusiasm. It is hard to teach people. It's even hard to teach the ones who are smart and keen to learn, simply because if you give them a trained horse they will untrain it and if you give them an untrained horse they will get hurt. That's why a horse that will consistently do its job as a lesson horse is completely worth its weight in gold.

Darius and I got on fine. I may have had a bit of a crush on him - he was older, and he was brilliant with the horses. What's not to love? Well, at the time he was married and I have my own rules for that kind of stuff. Not that I'm a religious person, but good morals do matter. He however saw me as a kid, and often treated me as one too. Once on a road trip he became tired of driving and had Ariel take over. He wanted the whole backseat to himself so he pretty much just lay on top of me. It was the most uncomfortable trip ever. I was afraid to move and I swear he did it on purpose. During the road trips he'd play head games with all of us. Ariel was surprised once when I bought a slice of pizza at a stop. I was hungry regardless of the deal that said Darius would feed us while we were on the road. But I would have starved to death if I had only listened to that.

Ariel warned me: "Don't take the pizza back to the truck; eat it here. You know how he is about junk food."

If he only knew what we ate when we were at our little house and not on the road! I ate my amazing smelling pizza in the truck and he glared at me until it was gone. I even ate the crust. When you work as hard as working students work there is no such thing as dieting; even when you're stuck in a truck for hours on end, you need to get the calories when you can! He bought us drinks often, and it was always diet pop. I began to like diet Coke and even started to prefer it over regular Coke. In his own way he was caring for us by being particular about our diets.

At this point in the story I will introduce Atlas... the one and only. He is a barn favourite as a lesson horse now. Anyone who rides him falls in love with him as he is smooth and makes riding easy. I try to avoid putting new clients on him first for this reason.

However, Atlas was not this way when I met him. Darius's matching set of Morgans were identical in every way. Their registration papers said that Atlas had a few white hairs in his whirl on his forehead, but we'd never seen them. As I have mentioned, the only way I could tell them apart was that Atlas's ears were just a little bit more pointy than Alastor's. They had originally been one of the chariot teams, but Atlas had an accident and had fractured a bone in his hoof call the coffin bone. This bone is named that way because in the olden days a broken coffin bone would be the end of a career and most horses would have been put down. But times have changed. Now a hoof can be put in a cast and the horse can be kept on stall rest. The coffin bone can heal to be just as good as before in some cases. When I was working in Nebraska, Atlas was no longer on stall rest nor in a cast. He was just beginning to go back under saddle.

One day Ariel and I were allowed to take the Morgans for a trail ride. We saddled up and headed out. I rode Alastor and Ariel rode Atlas. She led the way. A few minutes in at only a walk Atlas leaped sideways and threw in the craziest 360 degree spin. Ariel stopped him and then he pulled it again. Neither of us had a clue what Atlas had spooked at, and my horse Alastor just stood and watched. That was my first interaction with Atlas, and I figured with that kind of spin he was too much for me. I didn't opt to ride him very often if I wasn't required to. But one day I was. Darius asked for me to ride him and work him in the ring while he was working his mustang. The first thing Atlas did was aim a kick at me while I was trying to pick out his back legs. Great first impression. Once I was riding, Atlas spooked at the corner that stored equipment and I had to work through getting him over it by bending him away and pushing him forwards. He responded very well and within a few minutes stopped fussing over the "scary corner". Ariel's horse, a thoroughbred she owned herself, was very upset about the same corner. She worked on it the same way I had with Atlas, but eventually she gave up on that and decided to try a different strategy. She took her thoroughbred for a gallop and made him run, then once he was getting tired and wanting to slow down she let him slow down only in the scary corner. If he spooked sideways, she'd send him forward and work the other end of the ring until he was ready to settle again. He was a very hot horse but he was smart and soon figured out that it was much easier to stand in the scary corner than to gallop around away from it. He soon learned to love the corner. The lesson stuck and he only had to try it once more before he ignored the corner altogether. A lot of people might think that this is not proper training and that they should work their horse to gain its trust and not push it forward when it gets nervous. But a horse will work to get a release. The release taught him that the corner was a place to relax rather than tense. Not all training issues can be dealt with the same way, and sometimes thinking outside of the box will work better than trying to do a system of what has worked in the past. This is the same as teaching children math skills. I know I was one who you could repeat the answers to a hundred times; you could make up flash cards or show me charts; you could even make up a rhyme (8 times 8 is 64 shut your mouth and say no more). But I would not get it simply by memorizing the answer; I had to understand how to figure out the answer. If I couldn't understand, then I couldn't get to the answer. My classmates would often understand the math sooner than I would. I'd go home and work with my dad or a tutor and I'd still get confused until I could understand the whole thing.

Both Atlas and Alastor were for sale. Atlas wasn't sound enough to do chariot races, so they had decided to split up the team and sell them. I heard this during my last month's stay and I approached Darius to see if he would sell me Atlas. He agreed and continued my internship another month without pay in exchange for Atlas. He also agreed to truck the horse halfway across the continent when the March Can-Am was held in Ontario. I was thankful and thrilled to have a horse of my own at the Rodriguez's. Later that day Darius asked us to bring in the Morgans saddled up so that we could do some trick training. A new intern was there as well - Anna. She and I had become friends quickly since we were close in age and living under the same roof. Anna opted for Atlas and I took Alastor. During the training session Darius asked for us to switch horses. Somewhere in the mix he hadn't realized I hadn't started off on "my horse". He had gotten the two horses mixed up. He was trying to get me to lay down Atlas while I was riding Alastor. But Atlas, having never been taught that, was utterly confused as to why my whip was cueing towards his leg. Finally Darius came over and attempted to cue the lay down from the ground. He swore at me for not sitting tall, thinking that I was causing the miscommunication. Finally he said out loud, "Alastor!" I realized he had the wrong horse, and I quickly told him. He yelled at me for not telling him sooner and after a few minutes of being reamed out, I got off the horse and left. I left Atlas with Darius and went to the tack room, trying to convince myself not to break down and cry.

I have trouble with confrontation. I am a strong young lady but I have always been shy, and so people yelling at me is really unheard of. It doesn't happen often that someone is so upset with me that they actually yell. I cried and tried very hard to pull myself together while standing in the tack room and hoping he wouldn't come in. In a few minutes I had pulled myself together and he did come in. He tried to apologize. He saw where he was wrong, but he had been upset for nearly ruining a horse who had no idea what was being asked of him. I understood what Darius was saying. It was the equivalent of asking a first grader to do algebra and punishing them when they don't know it. Darius was very intense and direct. There was a table in the middle of the tack room and I was literally being pushed around the table, even though he was actually trying to apologize. I felt like a horse at liberty in his round pen. Finally, something Ariel had said to me clicked in: 'always look him in the eye.' So I did. As hard as it was, I raised my eyes to his. He instantly softened and stopped talking. Our fight was done and we moved on.

On the Road Again

ANOTHER BIG TRIP WAS AHEAD AND WE HAD BEEN packing the trailer for days. We weren't taking the whole crew, just Darius's truck and the four horses he needed for the performances. Ariel and I were going as the interns and Justin was coming along to help with the booth during the day and the sound during the clinics. It was a long 12-hour drive all the way from Nebraska to North Carolina. Darius didn't waste time and he drove his truck and trailer like I'd drive a sports car. However, when the temperature dropped below freezing Darius nearly slammed on the brakes and brought the rig back to just barely above the speed limit. That's a hard limit. Don't drive fast in bad road conditions. Thank god for that, not that I could ever sleep at all on the trips anyway.

We stopped at Alex Walter's place. This young man was astounding and positively amazing all round. I had first met him in Florida. He was nine years old going on ten. Alex had been born with half of his legs missing; he had knee joints but nothing below that. He was luckily born to a horse riding instructor who gave him the most amazing equitation seat you will ever see in a rider (of any age). This young man would keep crowds intrigued (even out in the rain) while he did a clinic just like his mentor, Darius. His school projects would be laying out his presentation on horsemanship. He was a wonderful speaker and a lovely person in general.

So back to the main story... We ended up stopping before we got to the expo in North Carolina to stay at Alex's farm. We arrived late in the evening and Darius joked with Alex's mom while we unloaded the horses and got them settled. Then we were given a bit of a tour. The facility was incredible with lots of gorgeous horses, large barns, an indoor arena, and a beautifully kept outdoor arena. It also felt homey. The barn was tidy and swept but the horses were happy for attention and were begging to be pet or fed. It was obviously a schooling barn but a barn I'd be proud to run. That's when I got a good vision for the future as my mind took a photo during this short visit. After the horses were settled, we ate chocolate fondue and were treated like royalty. There was a picture hanging in our room of a beautiful bay jumping a huge jump. It looked exactly like my Jake at home, and so I was instantly homesick. In the morning I asked Alex's mom who that horse was. It was of course her own pride and joy: Mystical Knights. I loved the name and hoped I'd meet him, but we were packed up and off to the expo before I knew it.

A friend of mine from college lived in North Carolina. Michaela was thrilled to hear I was going to be there and met up with me almost as soon as we had the horses settled in and the booth unpacked. Darius was kind and let me take off for hours on end through that expo to spend time with my friend who I hadn't seen since college. Ariel and I were able to relax quite a bit and enjoy the expo. We spent most of our time watching the clinicians work the audiences (or maybe it was the horses working the audiences - whatever way you looked at it). I absolutely fell in love with the announcer. He had also been the announcer in Florida and his deep kind voice was very welcomed every expo. Each expo we had a family on the road. There was an elderly couple who provided mats for Darius's booth and gates and panels for setting up round pens or stalls when needed. Rob Jimes and his wife were at nearly every event that Darius took me to. Rob was a lovely character: he was a priest, a horseman, and a husband. Another Cowboy Randy. You could just see that he loved to tell a story and I enjoyed listening to each and every single one of them. He often hosted cowboy church on Sunday mornings. At the hotel, Ariel and I would catch him talking aloud and flipping through his Bible while trying to put together his talk. I am not religious at all, but having gone to a Catholic school and attended Sunday school and quite a few church events I feel I understand the culture that is brought up with this. Good morals are hard to find. It is nice that churches continue to teach good morals and I respect that. I would go to cowboy church often just for the sheer companionship of the people. They were all kind and friendly, and you knew they all loved horses.

Ariel and I were first instructed to go out of our way to help Rob set up whatever it was he had brought. It was always heavy lifting and of course, with Rob being an older fellow, he wasn't really supposed to work as hard as he did. Once we met these fine people we didn't need to be prompted to help. We would see their truck pulling up and get right in there and ask what needed to be done. These are the people who would give the shirts off their backs to help others; they are the people who are worth fighting for. Rob Jimes runs a trail riding stable in Ohio and often hosts bigger events with horse training seminars and auctions. If you are ever in his area you should look him up.

Going to his ranch with some of my own horses and participating in a big event is definitely an item on my bucket list.

The North Carolina expo was pretty great; we only had the four horses to look after so chores were quick and effective. It was a small expo so Darius lived it up. He often led his horses around without their halters (just at liberty) to shock the people milling about the barns. He loved the attention. We were blessed with as many learning opportunities as were available. I got to see a Haflinger stallion jump over three feet during his demo which inspired me to train Portia to jump better. I was able to watch Tennessee walker horses do their thing, which honestly didn't teach me a lot, but it showed me that there were people having fun with lots of strange breeds. It wasn't just me with my crazy standardbreds; lots of other people had horses that didn't simply walk, trot, and canter like regular horses. Darius really enjoyed being in front of a crowd. He did every demonstration as if it was the one that counted. There was never an off day. In one demonstration he was showing the crowd how to lay a horse down.

He said, "It is so simple; all you have to do is cue, one knee, two knee, and then the hiney."

Later on, straight-faced, he asked the audience: "What is the difference between whoa, and hoe?" He stood there in silence and waited for someone to answer. Sometimes there would be a brave soul who would try to answer the question but generally they would just stare in shock, which I think he secretly loved. He loved making the audience uncomfortable. This was a joke that led him into the next part of his demonstration: "When you say 'Whoa,' you must absolutely mean Whoa. The horse should stand, and if it doesn't, you put it back. The second you see that horse shift its weight to take a step, you need to correct it, because after that horse moves its leg then you're too late to correct it."

As this was a slightly smaller expo Darius tended to use it for fun activities. He fell off during a Roman riding demonstration (that is when you ride standing up with one foot on one horse and the other foot on a different horse). He dusted himself off and exclaimed to the audience: "I don't know what you're all so worried about, that's the seventh time I've fallen off today!" It's not a big deal. Get over it, get back on, and do it better.

During one demonstration I was holding a horse for Darius while he worked another horse. He had spoken briefly before the demonstration that he wanted some horses to exit to give the other horses more room to work; however, he hadn't said exactly when he wanted those horses to leave. So we were there holding horses waiting for a cue to exit the ring. That cue may have been so subtle that it was missed, or else the lack of communication was just so that another helper and myself stayed inside the ring holding two horses. Darius was working with his mustang Bolt. Bolt eventually turned into an outstanding horse, he has been a stunt horse in many movies and has done nearly every trick in the book. Darius was working with him that day and we were holding onto the star liberty paint team (Taz and Topaz). Darius was working at liberty, which means no attachments. Bolt decided at that moment to have a wild mustang moment and took off bucking. He aimed a kick at the horse I was holding and got me instead. In front of 200 people I sank to the floor by the sheer impact. I wasn't sure exactly where I'd been kicked, but I stood up, smiled, and we continued the demo. I had a few tears running down my face, but I smiled. I was performing just like Darius; I was part of the group and I belonged there (regardless of the fact that Darius had wanted us to take the extra horses out of the ring earlier and we just hadn't known). An ambulance was called and the paramedics spoke with Alex's mom outside of the ring. She whispered, "Are you sure you're okay?" I nodded yes and the paramedics left. I did my damn best to not interfere with the demonstration. Later that evening I found a lovely bruise on my hip where my belt had been sitting, and another on my elbow. Nothing life-threatening and I was proud to say that I handled it. We got a short muffled grunt that those horses shouldn't have been in there and luckily the horse wasn't kicked. Wow. Darius wasn't known for kindness, but damn he was good with the horses. It hurt my feelings that he hadn't even asked if I was alright. I had respected him. Would I now? Probably not.

Maturity is something that takes time. I am always learning; I am always growing. If I wasn't, then I would become a stubborn old hag who always thinks she knows what is right. That is my worst fear. Let me learn, always. I will learn from every student I coach, from every horse I work with, and from every negotiation and social encounter I make; I will always learn more. If you don't, if you limit yourself, if you think you already know it and you've got it, then you have just stopped growing. That is the worst thing you can do to yourself. If you stop growing, you stop living.

At the time of writing, my grandparents are both in their eighties. They inspire me. They grow daily, they learn more, and they interact with others for the sheer sake of interacting. They go to lectures, they go to conferences, and they participate in politics, clubs, and all sorts of social events. They always learn from their experiences. They talk about theories, new practices, health, and wellbeing. They are my inspiration.

Please never stop learning. I don't care if you laugh at this book because it recalls a lot of unfortunate events, a lot of lucky events, and a whole lot of just living, but please take from it what you can. Be the person who never stops learning. You can always be better. Stay open-minded. The best horse trainers will always learn more.

At the North Carolina Horse Expo, Darius practically begged us to go and watch a young lady who was working with her horses. Ariel and I went, although we were a bit confused as to why he had chosen her for us to watch. He insisted that we would learn a lot from her, and rather than shopping or socializing or working the booth, the ring was where we should be. So we watched. We watched as two nervous horses ran from their owners, their trainer, and her assistant. We watched for nearly an hour. Using quiet and very subtle cues, she convinced the horses to trust her. The horses were flighty. They were Arabian-bred horses which are known to be hot, and they were in a new place with a lot of people and a lot of things to look at. There were banners, speakers, music, people coming and going, and horses coming and going. That is a lot to take in for a young horse. But the Arabians eventually started to work with their handlers. The handlers didn't chase flat out like I've seen a lot of cowboys do. Instead, they chased them a bit, turned them around, and gave them a chance to commit to the relationship. They kept saying over and over with their body language: "Hey, I'm in charge. Take it or leave it; I am leader. Look at me: I'm your person; I'm not going to hurt you." The trainers got down low and crouched on the ground. The flashy Arabians turned and approached them. They didn't necessarily get a true join up, but they got moments where the horses decided that they were a safe place. Bit by bit they gained the horses' trust. It was great to see. The trainer didn't talk a lot. Occasionally she explained why she was doing something, but for the most part she just focused on the horses and let us learn from watching. This stuck with me. I thought for a second maybe there is more to liberty, and then I understood it. There is more. You need to learn horse. You need to learn the language of the horse, rather than make the horse learn the language of the human.

Ruby

I HAVE DEVELOPED A METHOD BASED MOSTLY ON Darius's methods to train a horse to stay with me. At the time of writing I have found a horse who has stolen my soul. I knew from the moment I sat on her back that she was my horse, and she has made it her mission to try and teach me how to actually speak horse. She joined up with me the first day I worked with her on the ground by making perfect circles and following me no matter how fast I ran. As much as I want to understand horse, there is so much I need to learn. I feel like I have developed a method to communicate with the horse that is half speaking horse and half speaking human. It's a compromise. But what will happen when I get a truly wild horse who doesn't want to compromise, one who has no intention of learning the human ways? What am I to do then? Slowly, Ruby is teaching me. She is teaching me all that she can, and I am doing my best not to teach her any human. I have refused to teach my horse to lunge on a long line. I ride her, and she still doesn't know basic lunging. I am listening to her. She owns me. I am her student who is doing my best to learn for the sake of the horse.

Some people would call me crazy for even getting on a horse who cannot lunge. But I am learning to communicate without yelling. My body language sometimes yells. It doesn't mean to. Ruby shows me I've yelled by galloping away when my body is too aggressive. After years of round penning horses, you'd think I'd understand what is too aggressive and what is not. But it's not easy to learn a language. If you listen, it gets easier. Stop asking so much of yourself and your horse and just listen. A horse tells you so much. Basic signals like lowering the head means that they are either trying to see something close up or that they are relaxed. These are simple basics that we as humans should pick up on, but we don't. Very few instructors understand these concepts and even fewer actually teach them. A lowered head means that happy endorphins are going to the horse's brain, and that means the horse is in a great state to learn new things because they are not worried. They are not tense or fearful about what is going to happen next. This is not to be confused with horses whose heads are tied down in a low position. Just because they have become submissive to an aid (a training tool like a tie down or a martingale, side reins, or a harsher bit) does not mean that they are relaxed and in a state to learn. You must learn to read your horse. I start my students off with grooming and very basic things. For example, if your horse leans into your curry comb you're likely doing a good job brushing and they want to feel it a little harder. But if your horse moves away, then they are picking up on your nerves or maybe you are causing them dis-comfort in another way. Horses are very sensitive. I sometimes have students tell me that their horses like or dislike particular things. I try to be open-minded. Most of these students are very new to the game and are interpreting the horse's language very differently than I would. A horse that rubs against you does not treat you as an individual; you may as well be a fence post that is nice to scratch against. A horse that runs you over and leads the way definitely doesn't think of you as the leader; in reality they think of themselves as being superior and in charge.

Herd

HORSES NEED TO HAVE A LEADER AT ALL TIMES. THAT is the most important social skill they use to know who is leader and who is not. As prey animals, horses work in a herd to protect themselves. If they don't know whether the leader of the herd is capable of keeping them safe, then that is when all hell breaks loose. Each horse in the herd needs to know who is above and who is below. If they don't know, then they will spend every last ounce of their energy trying to figure it out. They will fight over food, over water, over companionship, and over space. Once they know who has their back, then life is good, life is simple. For example, Portia, as the lead mare in a herd of ponies, fights every step of the way to prove she is in charge and no one else. While Atlas acts as the "stallion" who gets to say when the herd should run from danger, don't get me wrong - the lead mare says how far to run, how fast to run, where to run, etc etc. Other than Atlas and Portia, there is Bella (cute little Welsh pony rescue mare); Chance (small pony gelding); and Charlie (large pony, likely a Haflinger cross who is very sturdy and opinionated). Portia spends literally all day telling Charlie who is boss. The others agree that Portia is in charge and there are no issues. Chance has even snuggled up to Portia and shared hay. The only issue is that Charlie would like to be "lead mare"; even though he is a gelding he would like to be in charge of the herd. He won't fight Atlas as he knows better. Atlas is obviously the horse no one messes with - Atlas is the stallion. Atlas would be the horse to take on the cougar or the mountain lion while everyone else in the herd would follow Portia to safety. Portia and Atlas are at the top of the herd together. Portia will allow Atlas to be in charge but Portia is really the brains of the operation. When the herd is running from something Portia says how far and how fast. Charlie isn't quite sure if Portia is up to the job, but Portia assures him that she is each and every day. She chases him away from the food, she chases him away from the water, she chases him away from the herd, and she generally just chases him. She says, "If you belong in this herd, then you need to start acting like it." It's typical of young male horses to act out and test authority. Portia has a few years on Charlie, and since Charlie is new to the herd and is pushing his limits within the herd, it is only natural for Portia to put him in his place. Once this order is in place, the herd will be settled. Everyone will know for sure where they belong, who has their back in case of emergency, and who they need to look out for. This is how a herd works.

Natural horsemanship is a term that has been used over the last twenty years or so to describe a calmer and easier way to train horses. This may or may not be the case. Natural horse interactions are not calm; they are abrupt and they are fierce and they are mean. They are quick and over with fast, but they are by no means nice and gentle like a lot of natural horsemanship trainers try to convince soft-hearted horse people to buy into. Horses in the wild give a slight warning followed by a very firm kick or bite. Don't like that? That's fine; natural horsemanship isn't for you. I say this almost jokingly. Many trainers have made their names by selling training systems and products that reflect very subtle and gentle horsemanship systems. I agree with that wholeheartedly. However, they cannot claim to be natural horsemanship experts as natural horse talk is very direct. The impact that follows a warning is why the horses respond to it. If a horse in a herd is at a hay pile eating and a young horse that is lower in the pecking order tries to join in, then the lead horse will say no. They will say no by swinging their heads with their ears pinned. The younger horse will accept that answer and back away. There you go; that's natural horsemanship. Watch it in the herd sometime. If for instance that young horse decided that the hay was worth the risk of the elder horse's warning and continued to approach the hay, maybe even stealing a mouthful, then the older horse would flat out charge at the young horse. If the horse didn't back off, then they would make contact and it would hurt. The elder horse may also decide to turn its hind legs to the younger horse and throw in an effective defense move. If you have ever taken a kick from the hind legs of a horse, then you know how much power a single kick can provide. I have.

Be the leader. Be confident, even if you have no idea what you are doing. Shoulders tall, eyes up, walk forward, and lead the way. The horse will follow.

Home Again Home Again

I SPENT A LOT OF MY TRIP IN NEBRASKA TRAVELING. Whether on the road with the Rodriguez clan or going to and from my actual home in Ontario, I traveled a lot. My first trip home was for my grandfather's funeral. My grandmother had passed away quite a few years previously, and now it was my grandfather's turn to fight cancer. He was fighting a losing battle, and when he passed I knew my mom needed everyone home. I wasn't as close to this grandfather like I am with my other grandfather, but at his funeral I cried and could not stop. He was a good father and a good grandfather; we just didn't live close to each other. But when we had time together, we had been close. It was very hard on the family to finally let him go. He fought as hard as he could to stay with us.

The night I came home, it was close to midnight by the time I arrived. I went to check on the horses and found Cricket very upset. I brought him into the barn and within minutes had called the vet. My father had done grain that night instead of my mom. He had measured out the grain completely backwards and Cricket had been overfed. The vet came. She pumped his stomach and then she put an IV in. Cricket was in so much pain that he had become aggressive. I had only seen him like that once before from a very severe muscle tear. I slept in the barn that night. In the morning I followed the vet's instructions and took his IV out. He was doing a lot better, but this was the worst colic experience I have witnessed.

My second trip home was for Christmas. First I got on a train that took me to Chicago. From the train I got diverted onto a bus due to the tracks being too icy to travel. The whole trip there was controlled by one angry, arrogant self-righteous man who was both Canadian and American and a regular traveler. He would not talk quietly and he would not stop talking. After a long trip I eventually made it to the station where Calabe picked me up and we crossed the border and drove home.

Christmas was great and Calabe and I drove back to the border a few days later to head back to Nebraska. But at the border we were singled out and brought inside. After a long wait, some fingerprinting, and loads of questions I became very ill. I'm not sure if it was a flu bug or if it was the anxiety that was caused by all the accusations I was receiving from the border patrol. We drove back to my parents' house and I crashed. For days I felt ill and then I finally got around to putting together documents for the border patrol so that I could cross and resume my internship.

I had to get a note from my boss at The Beer Store that said I had a job to go back to. My store manager didn't have enough authority to write the note and so I had to go to my district manager who had been switched while I was gone. I introduced myself, explained my situation, and he kindly wrote me a letter stating that I was employed and that my internship in Nebraska was basically a leave to learn just like a school program. Thank you, Brad! I had never met the guy but I was grateful! I brought that note with a lot of bank documents that said I could support myself on my own while I was there as an intern (to convince them I wasn't being paid and taking a job an American could potentially have). They let us cross. After a long drive back, I was finally in Nebraska again.

I learned a lot. It was four months, but it felt like four years. I made lifelong friends who I still keep in touch with, and the skills I learned I absolutely couldn't have learned in any of the programs offered in Ontario. Four months of pure work ethic, sweat, tears, and absolute love for the horse. I may have hated a lot of it at the time but I loved it as well, and I could never replace it. Internships are by far the way to go if you're looking to learn new skills. There are many trainers who will step up to the plate and teach you everything you need to learn if you work hard and prove to them you're worth being taught.

When I came back from Nebraska, now single and free, I knew what I wanted to do. It was as clear to me as it had been from the age of 14. I wanted my own farm and I wanted to train horses and coach people to ride and train better. I wanted to help bridge the gap between horse language and human language. I wanted to help create some understanding for humans so that they could work better with horses. I finally put together a plan. I would rent a farm until I built up my business and could afford to purchase a place of my own. In the meantime, I went back to working at The Beer Store to pay for my horses and pay off my school loan. I searched the classified ads daily by typing in all sorts of combinations trying to find anything within a two-hour radius that could support a business. I explored a few different farms. One man had an old lawsuit against him which came up very quickly on a Google search relating to animal neglect. He explained to me and my father when we were touring through what it was about. A previous tenant hadn't taken care of the animals, and because he was landowner, it had come back to him. Seems pretty unfair. Regardless, we steered away from that farm; it just didn't feel right. Good potential facility-wise, as it would have ran an epic horse camp with bunkers and lots of shower stalls. It had room for chickens and ducks, pens set up for all sorts of animals, and a petting zoo would have fit in just fine. But I got over it. It just didn't feel like it was the right place for me.

I was able to score a second job working as an after school co-ordinator at REACH Huron which is an equine facility so it was right up my avenue. I moved up to kids' co-ordinator and I also ran the open ride nights where I got to meet a lot of the horse people in the area. Some people came from as far away as Milton to ride in the arena. The arena was to die for. It was bigger than Olympic size with state-of-the-art footing, heated viewing sections for over 200 people, great lighting, and music! Not a lot of arenas even compare to this one. However, the job I had was wearing me down. I drove nearly an hour to get there each day, mainly worked with children (rather than horses), and then drove home. I organized camps and was in charge of registration and keeping track of payments. There was a lot of office work, but I wasn't working in the barn with the horses. I did get to coach for a while, but pretty soon they hired a certified coach and I was pushed aside. So I worked and I kept searching for a place of my own to rent.

Stratford

FINALLY I CAME ACROSS AN AD FOR A PLACE IN Stratford. It was affordable, and so I called and was able to view it pretty quickly. It was small and it was quiet. It had a double-gated entrance - not one gate but two. There was a third gate to get to the horses' area. That should have been my first clue that something was off - why were there so many gates? The accommodations weren't spectacular. I'd be sharing the kitchen and living room but I'd have my own small apartment downstairs. I loved the downstairs apartment. The carpets were thickly padded and so even though they were old, they cushioned your feet as you walked. It felt odd being below ground but I had my own bathroom, bedroom, and living area. In the barn I could use four or more stalls depending on how many horses the owner had. There was an indoor arena that was small but usable. There was more turnout than what was available at my parents' farm. There was also a beer store in town. I was able to transfer to the store and I moved in fairly quickly.

I quit my job at the REACH centre where I had worked for nearly two years, and I focused on building an English riding program. I offered boarding and horse training. I was one of the only lesson barns around, and I was most definitely the only English barn around. That gave me an edge, but it also put me at a disadvantage: there were no barns around because there weren't enough people to support it. I lived there for ten months. In those ten months I developed a small but reliable clientèle. I was training twenty students a week, and I always had at least one boarder and one horse in training. I was almost breaking even by the end of it; mind you, I was still working part-time at The Beer Store.

The downfall of Stratford was the crazy. Reflecting back there was a whole lot of crazy in that town: my landlord for one, but my boss at the store for another.

Crazy

THE BEER STORE ISN'T EXACTLY KNOWN FOR BEING clean, as it's a quick in and out for most customers. They are there to drop off a few empty cases and pick up a few full ones; often their transactions are complete in less than a minute. It's fast-paced and it's tiring. If all of your transactions took less than a minute, then your shift would fly by, but that wasn't always the case. We had customers who brought in thousands of empties and would walk away with hundreds of dollars while leaving our store scrambling to keep up with the next twenty customers and simultaneously trying to organize, pack, wrap, and move pallets or empties around in the back of the store to make room for more. One customer was twenty cents off in the count after a more than two hundred dollar transaction. Either I had missed two 10 cent bottles or she had counted two extra 10 cent bottles, but for less than a quarter and more than half an hour of my time in a busy store with other waiting customers she was furious. The customer is always right, right? Yes indeed, especially if they are crazy! Trust me when I say that I didn't want to give her those two damn dimes, but I did and without any fuss as we had a lineup and I wanted her out of the store. The next time around she brought her list, which she insisted I check back to and count aloud as I sorted her empties. Talk about slowing down the entire day. It's no wonder the rest of the employees would disappear when a van would pull up. Smoke breaks were a given; too bad I didn't smoke.

Our store was one of the older stores in Ontario, and as with most Beer Stores it was in desperate need of some TLC. With a moldy roof we finally got some attention and the roofers started working. The problem was that the employees didn't. Anyone see what was going on here? The employees were working while the roof that was full of mold was being taken apart and removed. Talk about a health and safety hazard. I walked in for an afternoon shift and one of my fellow employees told me what was going on. She said she was the safety person responsible for the store and that our boss wasn't listening to her. She was worried about her lungs (she was a smoker, but it's funny how that works). She was also worried about things falling in on us while we are trying to carry cases out of the cooler, which was under the main area of the roof that was being replaced. Then I did a very brave thing and went next door to Tim Horton's. I phoned our district manager, followed by the union rep for health and safety-related issues. My boss was livid. But my phone calls got the message across. We were given face masks and tarps were put up to prevent any pieces of roof from falling on us. It was better, but still a crazy work environment. We were literally wiping cases down before rolling them out so that the "dust" wasn't going out with the beer.

Crazy didn't stop there. The man I rented the property from was more than just the cherry on top. He was strange and had all sorts of odd behaviours that just made you ask why. He would panic if there were a few rain drops and rush the horses indoors.

He would be upset if I didn't rush my own horses in, and if I wasn't there he would do it himself, expecting gratitude. I am a firm believer in horses being outside, unless there is severe weather. He was not. This was a minor disagreement between the two of us. We started really having problems when he began setting up traps in my apartment. He was welcome downstairs as he had to do his laundry in the basement; however, traps were a bit over the top. He'd set tiny balls of paper on top of a door between the frame, then if the door was opened the paper would fall. This was smart, as of course most people wouldn't notice the paper. However, I did. I asked him about it and he said he was trying to catch my instructor's friends snooping through his things. He had a few storage rooms downstairs that were not part of my apartment. My instructor had friends drive her as she didn't drive on her own and her friends would often camp out in my apartment doing their work on their laptops or napping. That's when the signs of paranoid schizophrenia started to show in my landlord. He would later explain his theories to me about how his neighbour looked through his mail (his neighbour delivered mail for a living), how the government was out to get him, or how I had poisoned his horse to make her abort her foal. Read that last one again. He accused me of drugging his horse so that she would abort her foal. I would never do that to my worst enemy's horse! If I wanted to get back at him for something, I'd have drugged him, not his horse!

I knew he was crazy by this point, but I didn't leave. I wanted my business so badly. I wanted to create a career I could be proud of. I wanted to quit The Beer Store. I wanted to make a living doing something I love and something I am passionate about. So I stayed. I put up with him turning the lights out in the riding arena to save power. I put up with him drunk and singing at night. I put up with his crude jokes, and him spying on us from the hayloft where he would sit for hours and just listen to what was going on in the barn below. I put up with him accusing me, my boarders, and my students of many crazy unheard of things.

But I left when he said, "I have found someone who will sleep with me and clean up after me, so unless you're willing to do so you need to leave." Yes sir, I was out of there!

Searching

I SEARCHED FOR NEARLY TWO WEEKS TRYING TO FIND a place where I could move my herd and business without losing my students. But I couldn't find anything. I moved back home, defeated. I hated myself, I hated my situation, and although I was grateful for my parents for taking me in with my horses, dog, and cat, I was awfully rude to them. I got along so much better with my parents when I wasn't stuck living at home. I sent out resumes galore. I made up five different versions and printed off over 200 copies. I sent them out to every online listing and every store that might possibly consider me. I had a new plan. I was going to find something full-time, work my ass off, and save up to get a better start at a facility that I wouldn't have to share. I was looking for a lease-to-own option, but in the meantime I would step it up, bite the bullet, work at a job I hated, and make the most out of it. That meant barely riding at all, coaching only what I could fit in, and only coaching when the weather would allow as my parents' farm did not boast an indoor arena to ride in.

Finally I got an interview at a dairy farm. When I went out there the guy gave me one look and sent me packing. He barely asked me any questions at all, and didn't even show me the cows. That was frustrating, as I knew dairy farms paid well and I was good with animals. I just needed to learn the routines. I got another call a few weeks later for a much larger farm I had applied to. I was invited to an interview. I wandered around and eventually found the boss. George was a big tall guy whose voice was louder than I thought humanly possible. I didn't feel intimidated by him though; he was an animal guy and you could tell he loved what he did. He asked me a few questions while we were standing by the cows and one of the cows came up and licked me. I giggled and slowly pet her nose; she didn't mind. George pretty much hired me on the spot. He told me his wife was good at looking at a herd of cows and picking out the sore or the sick ones, and he said that'd be something he'd expect of me eventually once I learned what was normal.

I was worried about quitting The Beer Store. I had worked there since college for nearly five years. But George was able to match the pay and nearly triple my hours, so I gave my two weeks' notice and walked away. I enjoyed working with the cows. The hours were long (either late or early) and the job was very repetitive but I had a lot of learning opportunities. They did a herd health day every other week and had the vet in. It was almost like a big team meeting and it was great. While there was always going to be that one person you don't get along with, the team meeting forced you to. Grow up, step up, do your job, be accountable, or be fired. George rewarded good effort, and he didn't accept disrespect. If you didn't show up, you probably shouldn't show up. If you showed up, worked hard, and fixed something, then you were golden. George was by far the best boss I have ever had. He spoiled each and every single one of his employees rotten at Christmas. It started the first day of

December with coffee and whiskey (or Baileys). For Christmas I got a pair of really nice work boots that I have worn for almost three years now and still haven't worn through them. Anyone who knows me knows that I normally go through shoes in about two months.

George had an odd way of attracting crazies though. His employee record is definitely a book in itself. One of his employees didn't have enough money to insure his vehicle to get to work each day, and George had loaned him two weeks pay in advance so that he could put tires on and make it in. The young boy was a drop-out with a good heart but not much for brains. He didn't bother showing up for a few shifts. He was let go of course, but then he called a few weeks later and asked for his paycheck. George arranged a time for him to come pick it up right after the barn chores were finished and we had headed out. He also arranged for a friend of his who happened to be a local cop to keep an eye on the road for a car that wasn't insured. As I was leaving for the day, I passed the boy pulling into the driveway. Then a few seconds down the road I saw a police car slowing to turn into the farm's lane. The boy got his paycheck and was then written up with his vehicle impounded. Don't mess with George!

While saving every penny, trying not to drive my parents insane, and working at the dairy farm, I was still looking for that next step. For a trainer your options are pretty narrow. You can be born into it, which I wasn't. You can be given it, start with two million, and go from there, but again I wasn't. You can work for someone else, which generally doesn't pay well. Or you can risk all you have, work as hard as you can for as long as you can, and just do it yourself. That was my plan. I was putting in the time at a job I didn't love so that I could do what I wanted for the rest of my life. That sounds like a regular person's retirement goals, doesn't it? I toured through many options when I was trying to find a place. I met with lots of business owners who tried to help me put business plans together or throw ideas at me. I followed every lead I had on places for sale, places for rent, lease-to-owns, live on property barn manager positions, paid working student positions, and more. Any ad placed online I knew about. I had twenty business plans written up for different scenarios and properties. I talked to my parents, grandparents, and my boss George for mentoring and ideas. I went to business start up companies, credit unions, and farmer credit companies.

Then I found a barn right outside of Cambridge. It had more than twenty stalls, a riding arena, a house, a race track, and beautiful fields with large shelters. The house was small but updated, and it had an older apartment that would be suitable for overnight summer camps. It was literally minutes from town and the price was doable. The price wasn't ideal, nothing like I had paid when I was in Stratford, but when I punched the numbers into my business plans and spreadsheets it came out alright. I spent a few days really thinking it over and trying to decide if it was going to be the place for me. I went back for a second visit and really took my time looking over everything, talking to the boarders who were there, and trying to ask every question I could to the owner. It didn't take me long to get my heart set on it. It was going to work out, so I told the owner I was in. But after a week he hadn't replied to me. He needed to discuss things with his wife. Eventually he told me it was a no. He didn't want a lesson program there because of liability issues as they were owners of the property and could be sued if anything were to happen. I tried to explain that's why we get insurance, but he was set and they decided to lease out to someone who only planned to board horses instead.

Frustrated, I kept looking.

A Real Home

ONE DAY I GOT AN EMAIL IN RESPONSE TO ONE OF MY ADS.

She said, "I have just what you're looking for."

We set up a time to meet very shortly after. This property was in Milton with nearly 50 acres, 40 stalls, an indoor arena, a huge outdoor arena, a house, and two apartments above one of the barns. The previous leaser was claiming bankruptcy and had a date to leave in place. The landlords hadn't even listed the property yet as they had just happened to see my ad first.

I set up a meeting and went out right away to view the facility. I loved it. Over the next few months we hammered out an eight-month initial lease to get me started at the new property. They gave me a discount to help me with the start up costs for the first few months, but they also charged me for lots of small things like maintenance of their tractor and property taxes to name a few. I soon found out that running a facility of this scale was not an easy task, as the overhead was huge. However, I decided to go for it.

In August just after my birthday I was on my way to meet my new landlords and sign the official lease. They would be meeting me at a new Tim Horton's in Stratford by the mall. I figured it was across from the mall, and drove around trying to find it. I even turned my music down so that I could focus better on looking while driving. I couldn't find it, so I ended up turning around at the next light. As I came back through the lights near the mall I saw the Tim Horton's out of the corner of my eye. I quickly changed lanes and drove into a car beside me. Whoops. Tiny little grey car in my blind spot. It happened so fast that I wasn't sure if I had checked my blind spot or not. Regardless, I got a ticket and had a very rocky start to my important business meeting. Adrenaline coursed through my veins. Once the cop had left and my landlords had gone inside the restaurant to wait for me, I sat in my truck and I cried hard. It wasn't a bad accident. I had barely scraped the door of the other vehicle. My bumper was just a bit scraped, but what really frightened me was the fact that I had been careless and hadn't seen them. On top of that I was completely embarrassed. I was trying to present business plans and act mature for my age, and I got in an accident on the way to the meeting. Nothing good about that.

While I waited anxiously for September first to come around, I kept busy working at the dairy farm. My boss had timed it perfectly, as he was putting in robots and I would be out of a job as a milker. However, before I could leave I had to train the cows to go into the robots and to enjoy the process so they'd do it on their own. There was also the programming of the robots as they had to be set up for each cow as they all have different udders. The sensors on the robots needed to be set for the first go around. If the sensors aren't helped, then the robot just bangs around hitting the cows' legs and udders trying to find the teats - which isn't at all fun for a cow. The first day of pushing all the cows through was very difficult, especially with the older adult cows. They were very cautious and sometimes went into flight mode just like horses do. Occasionally this would happen when we were between them and a fence panel. The first day I ended up with an outline of the belt I was wearing imprinted across my stomach, hips, and back. After those nasty incidents I learned to climb up the panel quickly when they panicked. We also added wooden boards behind the cows who were really bad and would back up quickly. Although they were more skittish of humans in general, the young cows were fairly accepting of the robot as they figured out the food reward. One of the cows, Friendly was her name, absolutely loved the robot, and the first day she went through 20 times. The second day she went through 60 times. The robot kept track of each cow, however, and knew that they weren't going to be giving any more milk after their regular milking cycles. So while the cow was allowed in, then the exit would be opened without any food being given. Some cows like Friendly would still try regardless and would basically do laps around the whole barn each day, taking mouthfuls of her regular feed before heading right around the aisles back to the robot.

We spent long days training the cows; between me and three or four others we nearly slept at the barn. My boss and his wife fed us around the clock and kept the coffee coming. The first few days it was literally two people on each robot all day long, morning and night.

The very last day I worked at the barn I had mixed emotions. I didn't want to leave, and so I stayed a bit longer than my boss needed me to. At the end of the day he gave me the biggest hug I have ever gotten and I packed up my belongings and left. I said goodbye to a few of the cows and the farm dogs on my way out. Though I didn't want to leave, I was so excited for my next adventure.

Moving day came the next morning. I had most of my stuff packed in the trailer the night before. Will came with his trailer and loaded the horses, my best friend Alisa came with her truck, and we loaded tack and other barn stuff into both of our trucks. My parents loaded a lot of my furniture into their van. It wasn't long before we were off. Lots of my friends helped me move and unpack the horse equipment as well as my own belongings. It is incredible how much we moved in such a short amount of time. I never let it hit home that I was doing it, running my own place because I wasn't yet. I didn't own the land, and I could still have everything taken away just like before. There were no guarantees, so I couldn't let myself get attached to the idea I had been chasing all these years. Even if it was mostly real.

Finally ready to run the business, I tried a new approach. I tried to be skeptical. You may not believe me after you read the next few pages, but I really did try. I tried to listen to my gut when I welcomed each potential new client, new boarder, or new student to the facility. Trying to read people is about as hard as predicting the future, and I am no good at either. Everyone seems to have a great heart, but some people can seem like that and still do very awful things. I see the best in everyone. This is what makes me an excellent riding instructor, but it also makes me easy to manipulate, and an easy target.

Over the years I have learned to always have a contract and always have the person read it over and sign it in my presence. This is time-consuming and awful but it does help in the long run. This is one lesson I have learned.

My first real trouble boarder came looking for a place where she could work off part of her board. Her name was Brittany, but there were a lot of other things I'd like to call her. I was keen on the idea of having an employee of sorts, and she was desperate for a place to bring her horse. She told me how she had been at this facility before and how she had worked for the previous owners. She told me a huge story about how the place she was at now was not treating her nor her horse fairly. I took pity.

She came with her old thoroughbred gelding who was a hard keeper, had awful manners, and required constant attention for eye issues. I worked as best I could trying to text her the second I saw anything different in his eyes. I couldn't do the eye drops on him myself and didn't want to. He was heavily medicated nearly the whole time he was here for his eye issues. He was a confirmation of why thoroughbreds are not my breed of choice; although I try and try not to be breed-biased, I am. Thoroughbreds don't have brains or feet. This horse lacked in the brain department when it came to turnout, as the second he was through the gate he would bolt. It didn't matter who was leading him, and it didn't matter if you had a chain over his nose. The only way his owner could prevent him from taking off was by sneaking him a treat while she quickly removed his halter halfway through the gate. He was absolutely the most dangerous horse to turnout I have come across yet. His feet were another issue. He was shod on the fronts and my farrier suggested he go barefoot as they weren't competing and his feet looked like they needed a break from shoes. The owner had literally had shoes on him since she had bought him and had never tried to take them off. Of course, once they were off the horse went lame. Now my farrier being a responsible guy tried to come out and fix the situation, but not before the horse's owner went insane on him. Brittany spread it all over Facebook that he had ruined her horse and how he was a no good farrier. I had tried to help resolve the issue by actually communicating with Sam about how she was upset and her horse was lame, as she had never even bothered to resolve the situation with him. That only made matters worse.

In her view I was always the evil one who was playing behind her back, when actually I just simply wanted her horse to be sound.

I hired another coach. She was excellent. Her background was very much show jumper and she had a wealth of knowledge. She was a natural coach, and very likeable. But she was only with us for a few months before her boyfriend got an offer for the two of them to spend a year in Australia. Like anyone would, she took her opportunity.

That brings us right along to Kandice, who was our next crazy, and a friend of Brittany. Kandice found out that I was looking to hire another part-time coach. She along with three others applied for the position. It was a hard decision as no one was really as good as the coach I was replacing, and none of the coaches had the same riding or teaching style as myself. Kandice was hired on her confidence alone as a loud and outgoing person who just demanded attention and respect. I figured it would be a good contrast with myself. Theoretically, if students didn't learn well with me, then they'd potentially do better with Kandice. But two weeks into her employment I fired her. I tried to train her first of course, but she didn't understand that students weren't supposed to rely on reins for balance and for steering. I had insisted she coach them to use their legs to steer. When she wasn't able to do that, I had no choice but to fire her. It didn't put me in a good position without a part-time employee but there was no way I was going to let that backyard style riding come into my stable. She refused to meet me in person for two days. Then I finally fired her over text message after she wouldn't take my phone calls. After Kandice was fired, many of the students came up to me to tell me how glad they were she wasn't coaching them anymore. That was a bullet dodged.

However, I still had her drinking buddy Brittany to deal with. She hadn't paid her board, even though her board was reduced because she was working for me. She wasn't getting her hours in and I was doing more and more work while she was doing less and less. I was paying her bill for her horse to live, and doing all the chores on top. Finally, I said, "You need to pay or you're out by the end of the month." She didn't like that. She completely lost it on me, and then decided it was better to put her horse down. Brittany spent 18 hours at the barn crying against her horse and yelling at the students who were trying to do their regular routines. She blamed me. She kept telling everyone that the reason her horse had to be put down was me. At the end of the 18 hours, my friend took it upon himself to ask her to leave. She sulked and finally left. But once she arrived home she sent out a death threat to me in public across Facebook. At this time I called the cops. Messages from her boyfriend came in saying that if her horse was put down because of me, then my saddle would be destroyed. I let the cops see that one too. They went and talked to her. They explained why announcing such things was a stupid idea and told her that she was welcome at the barn because technically the horse was still hers; however, she had to abide by the curfew set by me. A few days later her vet showed up to put the horse down. I met the vet when she parked and asked to speak with her for a few moments. I explained the situation and told her I needed to know her opinion of whether this horse should be put down. The vet said yes, as his eyes would require a lot more surgery than his owner could afford and that it wasn't practical to try to keep him going at this time. I asked for a copy of her report. She wasn't able to do that without Brittany's permission, so I didn't get one, but the vet did assure me that the horse had been put down by the owner and by vet recommendation.

Reflecting on this now I feel like I was the scapegoat; I was the person Brittany could blame for having to put down the one animal that had been a staple throughout her life. I understood her feelings, but it didn't make it right. It didn't make it right for her to threaten someone's life. I was just trying to pay my own bills and cover the cost of boarding a horse that didn't even belong to me.

Brittany didn't stop there. She and her good friend Kandice went further. They talked to our biggest competition, they talked to my landlord, they talked to the SPCA. They told so many lies that the SPCA actually showed up, unannounced, thinking they were going to find dead horses on my property. They brought in not one but two officers, thinking I was a neglectful abuser. The girls had taken absolutely anything they could find and made it huge and lied about it. They had told them we were using broken helmets in our program. When we checked out that allegation, we found one broken helmet. This was a planted helmet that had been in the "for sale" stall with its $5 price tag for decoration only. The SPCA saw fat, shiny, healthy horses. We exchanged numbers and they joked about taking all my fat horses off my hands for me. It turns out my farrier had worked with them quite a bit to rehabilitate neglected horses. So I showed them my own rescued horses and told them their stories. Some of my horses have come a very long way.

The SPCA is a very serious thing. If you get caught with anything that is considered neglect or mistreatment, then you can be charged enough to be put right out of business. I got a warning for water troughs as they had some algae built up. We changed our policy for water bowl cleaning during warmer months and have taken care of this issue. If we ever get another call that they come out for, we could be shut down as this would be the second call, thanks to those two fine ladies. The first call had come from Brittany who couldn't afford board or surgery to make her horse better. Let's just let that sink in a bit.

We had a third crazy show up not much later. She was a certified crazy, as she actually had a doctor's note saying she was too crazy to return to her job. However, she had purchased a horse, her very first horse, and had decided I was the best place for them to board. She was a talker and I didn't like that as she would talk for hours and it would be very hard to get away from her chatter without offending her. Soon she wrapped herself up in all things that she could. She wanted to change the sign, plant flowers, help with barn chores, get her kids riding, and take lessons herself. I would constantly justify her behaviour, telling myself that she was a new horse owner who thought she knew about things but she didn't, so at least I could help her by teaching her. But have you ever tried to teach someone who does all the talking?

It doesn't turn out very well. Even though I knew everything about her, her kids, her ex-husband, her cop friend, her favourite places to eat, even though she considered me a friend and wanted to be a part of every going on at the barn, she was still crazy. Her horse was moved to a different paddock one day and injured herself. I got the call from the coach who was working and I called the vet and the owner right way. Then I raced home to help in whatever way I could. The horse had cut herself across her forehead. It could have been a kick, a nail, or a tree branch for all we knew. The point was that it happened, it was caught fast, and it was cleaned and treated very quickly. The vet was there within twenty minutes and had her stitched up and ready to go in no time. The next day my boarder walked the fence. She didn't find anything but claimed she found hundreds of things. She took pictures of loose nails, tree branches, rocks on the ground, you name it. She then insisted that I pay her vet bill. I responded with, "If I pay your vet bill, then you're out of here by the end of the week."

I am not very good at handling crazy people. I just seem to make them more upset.

She went ahead and pulled a Brittany Round Two. She called the SPCA, she called my landlord, she called everyone she knew and told them what an awful place this was. She planted nails on paddock boards beside the gate. These were fresh shiny silver nails in the middle of a board and nowhere near a post. She took pictures of those and sent them to the SPCA. Thankfully the SPCA knew she was full of it. My landlord strongly suggested I pay her vet bill to shut her up. I took her advice, as she had dealt with situations like this before. She said it's just better to make problems like this go away. I didn't want to pay it, not at all, as it was simply not fair. If my horses are hurt, I pay for them. I am responsible for my horses. If I had a child and they got hurt playing in a playground with other kids, then I would not go to the playground owner and demand that they fix my child. I would not go to the parents of other children and demand that they figure out who had caused the accident. This was simply an accident, and horses will be horses. They play, they put their heads between fences, and they sometimes find something to get hurt on. One of Cricket's most serious injuries was caused by another horse stepping on his heel during play time. It took over a month of daily scrubbing, disinfecting, and bandaging to get him back on track. As a 14-year-old I knew it wasn't the other horse's fault and the other owner had absolutely nothing to do with it. My horse, my responsibility. What a weird concept of blaming others for something that was not in their control. I do fence walks regularly to make sure that there are no broken boards or fences down. I make sure the horses do not end up on the road. I am very cautious of their safety and I check on them multiple times a day, even if they are strictly on the low budget outdoor board. After this incident we did a huge overall of the fences, as they were fences that had been up for years and years. We weren't holding them in with dangerous fencing such as barbed wire, but surely bubble wrap wasn't a practical solution either. I paid a lot of money to have them updated. Older boards were replaced and absolutely any nail heads sticking out even a little bit were hammered in or pulled right out. I took no chances. If there is even the slight chance that I am at fault for a horse being injured, I am not happy with myself.

Had enough crazy for a bit?

I sure had.

I felt paranoid, like I couldn't trust anyone. Whenever there was even a slight complaint from a boarder, my heart would go through the roof. I wouldn't sleep wondering if they were planning to try to shut me down like the past two had. My anxiety was at its worse, and I almost decided on no boarders at all. I don't make very much money off of boarding horses, and if I actually calculated the time I spent looking after each horse there was no way to even make a living on an hourly wage. Without growing your own hay or owning your own property, boarding horses really isn't a money-making business. I knew that after crunching just a few numbers in my first few months of business. Once I had so much trouble, I knew it really wasn't worth pursuing. My goals kept going back to what I am good at. Teaching horses, teaching humans to teach horses, and helping humans and horses to build partnerships and communication.

I have met a lot of very special individuals in my days of coaching. Most of my students are an absolute pleasure to coach.

One of my students, a small nine-year-old boy on his very first day, was riding Cricket. He was very determined to trot and not do so much of the slow stuff. I convinced him that he had to learn to steer and stop and go before he could just take off.

Frustrated, he finally asked: "What makes you in charge?"

I said, "Well, it's my stable."

He said, "You don't own all the horses!"

I said, "Yes I do."

He said, "You don't own the barns!"

I lease, but I didn't want to give him the satisfaction of being right, so I responded, "Yes I do."

He responded with "You're only like what, 27?"

I responded with "26."

"No way," he exclaimed.

He made my day. This is the type of conversation I might occasionally have with an adult, but definitely not with a child. But he really got it, and maybe I inspired him a bit. You start to notice the children who are really keen. These are the kids who will make good business owners. They ask questions and they challenge, so you know that they will continue to grow.

Ontario isn't known for having extreme weather - okay, maybe in the winter, but not in the summer. This past summer, however, was the exception for us. We had quite a few storms that were legitimate light shows. They were so intense that I stayed up through the night and walked fences afterwards, checking that the outdoor horses were okay. One day in particular we had tornado warnings all over the province. Everyone was keeping a close eye on the weather and on the sky. We were supposed to get two storms, one at six p.m. and another at one a.m. The six p.m. one rolled through right on time, and I got some wicked cloud pictures with my panorama setting on my phone. It wasn't insane, but there was quite a bit of rain and then we watched the big storm cloud go around us. I went back to my daily chores. We didn't bring in horses early, and lessons continued throughout the evening. My last lesson of the day started at eight p.m. I even joked with them that they were brave venturing out with the storm warning still in effect. They had walked 45 minutes from the closest bus stop and this was their last lesson, so they hadn't wanted to miss it. They rode and we ended the lesson a few minutes early as I had started seeing lightning through the arena windows. There was no rain, just lightning in the distance. As the students untacked and groomed their horses, the lightning increased. I was getting worried about having to bring in the rest of the horses alone, and they were getting worried about having to walk along the road back to the bus stop. I made a suggestion that we do the buddy system: they could help me bring in the last few horses, and I would drive them home. They happily agreed. We stood at the door of the barn and watched the lightning, trying to judge how close it was and if it was safe to venture out. There was no noise, no thunder, and no cracks of lightning bolts. The lightning was going across the sky and looked like it was in the distance, even though it was all around us. We decided it was safe to go, and the three of us headed out to get Ruby, Portia, and Atlas. I got them haltered quickly myself as my students were still fairly beginner. Then I passed them each a horse and grabbed Ruby for myself. We headed back and the wind started to pick up.

I yelled out, "Walk fast but don't run," as I did not want the horses to get excited.

Halfway between the old barn and the main barn the weather went completely insane. The wind was coming sideways at us. It started pouring, tree branches were being thrown towards us, and cardboard and trash was spinning in the air. All three horses spooked and bolted sideways and backwards. We held them for a second or two and then with another gust everyone had to let go. The horses ran. Atlas ran straight for the barn, and the girls took off behind us. We too ran as fast as we could into the barn. Atlas disappeared in the barn as the wind came in on both sides. We could see the barn but we couldn't see inside the barn. The wind coming in on both sides had made the inside of the barn go completely white with dust from outside. When we got in, I had nearly lost my voice from screaming and cursing. The students I was with were white with shock. I quickly found that Atlas had made it to his stall and so I removed his halter and locked his door. I went to the tack room with the others but then noticed there was a car at the gate. It wasn't just that; they had the gate open and were just sitting there. I panicked again. I had two loose horses and someone was sitting idling with the gate wide open. I ran as fast as I could through the rain and found it was Lori who lives in one of the apartments above the barn. I yelled to her that there were loose horses and between my tears begged her to drive through. She had been scared to get out and close the gate with the branches coming down in the storm. I quickly shut the gate and then asked her for help bringing in the horses. She told me she would, then went upstairs and texted me that I was crazy to want to go out there. She came down once the storm had settled and we were able to bring in the other horses who had run back to their pasture and were luckily unharmed. Adrenaline still pumping and nearly without a voice, I drove my clients home and then drove home myself. I laid awake waiting and watching the weather forecasts, praying we wouldn't get something else when one a.m. actually came around. Thankfully we didn't, and I finally fell asleep.

At around seven a.m. I woke up to my phone ringing. One of my students whose mother works at the dog kennel (also on the same property) was calling to let me know there had been a tornado. I was well aware. I guess no one else was though. The young girls who were opening up the kennel for the morning showed up to fences down, branches through their building, and trees everywhere. They were utterly shocked. My landlord called to see if my roof was still attached. I explained to him what I knew and that I hadn't yet seen all the damage outside.

First thing I did was tack up Portia and ride her down the fence lines; she was the most shaken from the storm. The night before she hadn't touched her hay and that is very unlike a Haflinger pony. I knew she was the horse that needed to go and help me inspect the fence lines. She was very nervous heading out, but eventually settled into her task. We met up with one of my working students and her husband who were also out walking the fence lines.

The day was filled with people volunteering and cleaning up. Environment Canada came by to check out the damage, as did the local news channel. I ended up getting interviewed and was more nervous about that then I was about the actual storm.

I know that I have a very special person watching over me and keeping me safe. There are no other explanations for how I have experienced and survived so much in such a short time. My mom and best friend both say I have an army watching over me. This may be true.

By now I shouldn't be nervous. I shouldn't be nervous about anything. I am often the first person to sit on a horse's back. I can manage a group full of children for summer camp, all week long. I can drive. I can run my own business. I have ridden at top speed in front of a full audience on a horse without a bridle.

I was once a young girl who had never had a riding lesson. I lived in the city, and I dreamed. My dreams became bigger, my bucket list grew longer, and even though I am still sometimes nervous, like the young girl I once was, I know that I will continue to grow. I will become a better human. I will become more forgiving, more confident, and more including. When you are worried about being shy, you might forget about all the others who are feeling that way too. They need you to stop being about yourself. They need you to be about everyone.

Dreams are never a bad thing: they drive you.

I will never stop becoming a better horsewoman. If I reach my goals, if I go right to the top, and I represent Canada at the Olympics, I will still not be done. I will continue to learn.

Lightning Source UK Ltd.
Milton Keynes UK
UKHW040005301218
334695UK00001B/64/P